P9-DNQ-006

Praise for *The Wisdom We're Born With*

Reading this book is like having a great conversation with a deeply wise, kind, and supportive friend—who also happens to be an extraordinary therapist whose own losses have been profound teachers. With humor and grace, Dr. Gottlieb helps readers come home to their own natural inner wisdom, strength, and peace.

—*Rick Hanson, PhD, author of* Hardwiring Happiness: The New Brain Science of Contentment, Calm, and Confidence

Imagine one of your dearest friends sitting before you, sharing stories about the people he's loved, the people he's worked with, and himself, all at critical moments in their lives. With poignancy, vulnerability, and honesty, he moves you from laughter to tears to questions to insights. And you are so entertained, and so prompted to re-examine your own life, you just keep saying, *Tell me one more.* Dan Gottlieb is that friend, and in this tender-hearted book of transformative tales, he will tell you those stories.

—*Rachel Simon, author of* Riding the Bus with My Sister

Dan Gottlieb is not only openhearted, courageous, wise, and compassionate, he is also funny and irreverent. *The Wisdom We're Born With* is a book that teaches us how to live. There are no platitudes here, no easy answers. But the way Dan shares his life, including his vulnerability, gives readers the strength to face their own deepest pain and the inspiration to delight in every possible joy.

—*Ellen Bass, poet and co-author of* The Courage to Heal

Magically, Dr. Dan Gottlieb turns personal narrative into a reflective mirror that helps us discover and celebrate our inner selves. No wonder he is America's healer. Beautifully written with deep insights from children, patients, and friends, *The Wisdom We're Born With* is a model of how to live more fully in our fast-paced 21st century world.

—*Kathy Hirsh-Pasek, PhD, Stanley and Debra Lefkowitz Faculty Fellow, Temple University, and author of* Einstein Never Used Flash Cards *and* A Mandate for Playful Learning in Preschool

Reading this book is like having a loving, understanding, and good-humored friend remind you of what is most important in life. Drawing from his own journey and his clinical work with others, Dr. Dan Gottlieb's beautifully written stories of vulnerability and awakening illuminate the pathway home to our own wise hearts.

—*Tara Brach, PhD, author of* Radical Acceptance *and* True Refuge

The
WISDOM
We're
BORN WITH

Restoring Our Faith in Ourselves

by

DANIEL GOTTLIEB

Foreword by Daniel J. Siegel,
author of *The Mindful Brain*

STERLING ETHOS
New York

PASADENA LIBRARY, FAIRMONT
4330 Fairmont Pkwy
Pasadena, TX 77504-3306

STERLING ETHOS
New York

An Imprint of Sterling Publishing
387 Park Avenue South
New York, NY 10016

STERLING ETHOS and the distinctive Sterling logo are registered trademarks of Sterling
Publishing Co., Inc.

© 2014 by Daniel Gottlieb

All rights reserved. No part of this publication may be reproduced,
stored in a retrieval system, or transmitted in any form or by any means
(including electronic, mechanical, photocopying, recording, or otherwise)
without prior written permission from the publisher.

ISBN 978-1-4549-0639-1

Library of Congress Cataloging-in-Publication Data

Gottlieb, Daniel, 1946-
  The wisdom we're born with : restoring our faith in ourselves / by Daniel Gottlieb.
    pages cm
  ISBN 978-1-4549-0639-1 (hardback)
  1. Conduct of life. 2. Happiness. 3. Perspective (Philosophy) 4. Self-realization. I. Title.
BJ1521.G63553 2014
158.1--dc23
                              2013030254

Distributed in Canada by Sterling Publishing
℅ Canadian Manda Group, 165 Dufferin Street
Toronto, Ontario, Canada M6K 3H6
Distributed in the United Kingdom by GMC Distribution Services
Castle Place, 166 High Street, Lewes, East Sussex, England BN7 1XU
Distributed in Australia by Capricorn Link (Australia) Pty. Ltd.
P.O. Box 704, Windsor, NSW 2756, Australia

For information about custom editions, special sales, and premium
and corporate purchases, please contact Sterling Special Sales at 800-805-5489
or specialsales@sterlingpublishing.com.

Printed in the United States of America

2 4 6 8 10 9 7 5 3 1

www.sterlingpublishing.com

Contents

FOREWORD

You have in your hands the wisdom of a life well-lived from a man of extraordinary courage and creativity, humility and humanity. Dan Gottlieb's gift to us all is to put into words the deepest essence of how to bring meaning to our lives, to illuminate not only what really matters, but how to find gratitude and generosity in the common challenges of everyday living.

For those new to Dan's life story, let me simply share with you that his first third of a century was filled with reflection and appreciation, a keen sense of what it means to be a human being in a complicated world. He felt the common sting of not quite fitting in that many of us experience, and then found a passion that drove him forward—in Dan's case, the way of a healer as a psychotherapist.

But in the second third of a century of his life, we find our narrator at a very different moment in his journey. Following a nearly fatal car accident, Dan's broken neck left him paralyzed, with no movement below his chest yet a full range of experiences open to his keen and curious mind. After many tragedies and triumphs, Dan's life experiences have given his magnificent mind both a challenge and an opportunity to sense the extraordinary within the ordinary of our common routines that most of us in our busy lives often simply take for granted.

These life experiences have offered up to our wise author an endless set of challenges that have inspired unique reflections that most of us will never experience and learn from. But with Dan's writings, we are given the gift of his journey, the wisdom of his life.

Treasuring this amazing privilege of being alive becomes the teaching that Dan shares with us through stories of his own and others' struggles in their day-to-day lives. Simple narratives about people are surprisingly complex in the depth and power they bring, opening us to new insights and life-affirming reminders of how to live a life more freely and more fully. These stories help us liberate ourselves from our habitual thinking and give us perspective on what really matters in the face of unexpected traumas. This is the banquet of inspiring life lessons *The Wisdom We're Born With* serves up for us.

Being open to those tender places of vulnerability inside, which many of us either hide or have forgotten, is revealed as the essential step in finding a life of meaning and compassion. This way of being kind—of what can be considered a way of honoring and supporting one another's vulnerability—is the only way we can truly know and love one another.

Recent scientific research, some of which Dan explores beautifully in the book, highlights the neuroscience behind how living a life of compassion and meaning, connection and equanimity, creates positive changes even in the ways our genes are expressed to fight off disease and keep our nervous systems well honed. And so the wisdom we learn from Dan not only helps our minds feel better, it helps our relationships and our bodies live better.

For me, Dan Gottlieb has become an openhearted guide who reminds us all of the wisdom of being fully present for life. I actually read the book twice; I loved so much the feelings and the learning it has created inside of me. And now I am honored to let you know about what is in store for you as you open yourself up to Dan's wisdom, which I do not think will be the final words we hear from this marvelous human being and life-changing teacher. Enjoy!

—Daniel J. Siegel
Author, *Brainstorm, Mindsight, The Developing Mind,* and
The Mindful Brain, Clinical Professor, UCLA School of Medicine

INTRODUCTION

Phillips Restaurant was just outside Pleasantville, New Jersey, where I lived for the first seven years of my life. It was your standard family-style restaurant of the early 1950s—quietly busy, a place with white tablecloths and Frank Sinatra or Tony Bennett music in the background. And in that restaurant, there was a star attraction. Her name was Polly.

Polly was a large parrot in a cage in the middle of the lobby. In hindsight, I realize the owners of the restaurant probably put that parrot there to attract young kids. The ploy worked beautifully. Whenever my parents said we would be going out to dinner, I always asked to go to Phillips Restaurant because I knew I would get to hang out with Polly.

On the night I want to talk about, when I was about eight years old, my parents, my thirteen-year-old sister, and I went to Phillips with both of my grandmothers. (My grandfathers had both died several years earlier.) Once we settled in and started to look at the menu, a very heated discussion ensued among the adults. The discussion was about fish. Some fish, they said, were "too fishy," which is not good. (To this day I don't understand why having a fishy fish is a problem. We don't complain when a chicken is too chickeny.) Anyway, as the conversation became more intense, my mother and father and grandmothers continued to debate how some fish might have bones and others might be too spicy. None of this made much sense to me. That was okay, because a lot of adult behavior didn't make sense to me (still doesn't). But everything changed when my sister weighed into the argument. As a brand-new adolescent, she was trying to be adult-like. She joined in—offering her opinion about the fish.

At that point, I left the table and went out into the lobby where I could hang out with Polly (who really did eat crackers). Polly cocked her head from side to side, a bit curious about the kid down there below her cage. Meanwhile, the discussion continued at the table I had left behind. Out there in the lobby, standing next to Polly, I looked back at that family. It was my family, yes. And yet there I was, somewhat different from my own people. I didn't feel bad or good—just different. I wasn't fully aware of what this experience was or what it meant, but in hindsight this tiny little event was quite significant. I was to have this experience many times over the course of my life.

❦ ❦

I begin with little Danny Gottlieb in Phillips Restaurant because, looking back, I think it was my first awakening.

We all have first awakenings. There is that moment when we realize that even though in many ways we are like other people, we really are not. There is an existential aloneness—a sense of being completely apart from everybody else—that is almost overwhelming. For me, the questions began right there in Phillips Restaurant when I thought, *Who am I? Who do I belong to—if not these people?* Of course an eight-year-old brain is too young to wrestle with existential questions, but I did have a visceral sensation that evening. No thoughts that I can recall, just a visceral sensation.

Sixteen years later, I had that same sensation again. I had just landed my first job as a psychologist on a small, locked psychiatric unit in a general hospital in southwestern Philadelphia. Because it was a community hospital, we had all kinds of patients, including substance abusers, people with depression, and people with major mental illnesses like schizophrenia.

There I was with my first professional peer group—psychiatric nurses, social workers, art therapists, and others. But I was uncomfortable in case conferences where we talked about patients as "those people." I had gotten to know some of my patients very well, and in many respects I could identify with their vulnerability. And even though I couldn't verbalize it, I could identify with their alienation. I got to see them for who they were beyond their labels. Not so for my new colleagues.

So there I was again, watching "my people" but feeling different at the same time.

But now I was able to raise those big and often unanswerable questions: "Who am I? Where do I really belong? Who are my people?" Being young and insecure, I felt a kind of confusion and anxiety. But in hindsight, I also was aware of something that felt true and familiar. Another awakening.

Despite these brief awakenings, I still had a wish to belong—to feel like I was part of the group. I worked hard to realize that wish, living up to all of the expectations of the young husband, father, and psychologist. But still I had that familiar yet uncomfortable feeling that although I looked and acted the same, I was different. And so I worked even harder.

Until . . .

December 20, 1979, when I was in a car accident. I became a quadriplegic. Somehow in the midst of the blinding shock of this new world I had been thrust into, I knew I would never *belong* in the way I wanted to. I had known this my whole life, but never *really* knew it until that moment.

Now, more than thirty years after that accident, part of me is still standing out in the lobby next to Polly in Phillips Restaurant. I have spent my life looking over my shoulder at the family of humanity and feeling profoundly different. And yet, I know every human has the wisdom to know that truth. According to some Jungian analysts, the divine child is always an orphan. I am surrounded by my fellow humans, all of whom want to connect and belong (as we are social animals). And each one of us is an orphan child, living with the ongoing dialectic between wishing to belong and knowing we are different.

That day in Phillips Restaurant, I awakened to a certain kind of wisdom—the wisdom that I will be talking about throughout this book—the wisdom we are born with. My awakening could not have been taught to me by any teacher or drawn from any text. It was a combination of bodily sensations and circumstances that conspired to awaken me to a wisdom that I already carried inside.

I awakened—then I fell asleep again. As a young child, I could not hold on to such a realization. It would have overwhelmed me. So that insight lasted just seconds.

I believe this is what we all do. We have the wisdom, we carry it inside us, from time to time we awaken to it—and yet we fall asleep again. Sometimes it happens because we are not ready or we can't tolerate it, and sometimes it's because we are clutching so tightly to our belief system about what we should do and who we should be, that we are not open to new discoveries about our lives. So this wisdom goes underground. But if all goes well, we'll remember this wisdom in later years—when we can open up our hearts and our minds and can hear the very wise and quiet truth that we carry.

The book you are about to read is dedicated
to the Khulani Special School in rural South Africa
for Mduku children with multiple disabilities—the most
loving and grateful children I have ever met. More than
most, they embody the wisdom we're born with.

❀   ❀

PART 1

✳

Growing Up

THAT FIRST SCARY STEP
INTO THE FUTURE

Remembering so well that experience of a first awakening, I am always curious about the experiences of very young children. How do they begin to figure out who they are? When do they awaken to the possibilities of their own independence? What do they learn from others, and what knowledge do they carry within themselves from birth?

As I have been writing this book, I have been able to spend a lot of good time with Jacob, who has taught me a lot about how he sees the world.

I call Jacob my "virtual grandson," and with reason. Jacob's mother, Amy, is twenty years my junior. She and I have been good friends for fifteen years, and for many of those years, she has sometimes felt like a daughter or younger sister—but has always been a good friend.

When we first met, Amy was thirty years old and we spoke about her difficulties with her then boyfriend and about other issues that were deeply personal to her. She shared her vulnerability and, as a result, I have always felt close and somewhat protective. When Amy got into a relationship and became pregnant, I found myself anticipating the birth of her child as much as she did. And when Jacob was born, I rushed to the hospital to watch this newborn in the same way I had rushed to the hospital thirteen years before to see my precious grandson, Sam. Almost immediately, Jacob felt like another grandson to me. Not only did I feel a similar kind of love that I had felt toward Sam, I also felt devoted and protective. This child was family.

Amy's relationship with Jacob's father didn't last, and a few months after Jacob was born circumstances forced Amy and Jacob to move in with me. She didn't hesitate to ask, and I didn't hesitate to agree to have her move in. It's always been that kind of relationship.

And this was the first time in my life I was able to spend time with a little one as he grew. When my own children were babies, I had been too busy working to spend much time with them. And my own grandson, Sam, and his parents live some distance away from me, which meant I only saw Sam during visits. So when I watched Jacob take his first step, it was an experience I had never had before, and one I will never forget.

When Jacob celebrated his first birthday, he had no idea what was going on (something I can foresee in my future), but he did taste cake for the first time. He loved it.

It was apparent to me that Jacob had read all the books on developmental psychology, because was doing everything he was supposed to do at the right time—crawling, babbling, fingers everywhere. Now, adorable, happy Jake was ready to stand on his own. Most parents remember when their children first pull themselves up on furniture and—with wobbly legs and a wobbly head—just look around, so proud of what they've done. That's precisely what Jacob did.

Within a few weeks, as Jacob made further progress, he began trying out other moves. He would stand next to the furniture, let go for a few seconds, and then plop on his butt and giggle.

A week or so after that, he was *ready*. It happened when he was at my house with his babysitter and decided he would pull himself up on her leg. A few seconds later, he let go of her leg. She took a step back. And there he stood, wobbling a bit, with eyes as wide as saucers. Jacob reached out his hand for her to secure him, but she didn't take it. Instead, she held her hand just beyond his grasp.

As I watched this awesome event for the first time, I could barely breathe. This moment felt monumental in his life as well as mine. There he stood, unsteady and looking for security from someone he trusted. He slowly began to sit down on the floor, and then, before his diaper made contact, he righted himself and again reached out to the babysitter. But she merely encouraged Jake to take the step necessary to reach her hand. I watched as his eyes and his little chest seemed to be moving rapidly. I wanted desperately to save him from his distress.

Then it happened, just like we knew it would: He took his step. We all applauded. My eyes welled up with tears.

Perhaps you've observed what comes next. Perhaps you've experienced it yourself, as an adult.

In the Hebrew Bible, God says to Abraham: "Leave your father's house." In effect, *leave what is familiar*—leave what you have known to be home in order to begin the journey of your life. Neurologically speaking, that's what Jake did. He chose not to sit down and crawl. He embarked instead on the unfamiliar, having no idea what would happen. In the process, he literally took the first step in his journey of life. Letting go of what's familiar, whether it is leaving a babysitter's hand or leaving a father's house, is always an act of faith. We are always frightened when we let go.

To grow, we must release our grasp on the familiar. There is no easier way. Abraham had to leave his father's house. The rest of us must leave the narrative we've spun for ourselves—the story of who we are, how and why we feel the way we do, and what we need in order to feel better or happy or secure.

When I listen to married couples, I often hear such stories. For instance, the wife may say she has been in a marriage without love and can't live that way anymore. She says her husband is not capable of the kind of love she needs. She says she has tried for many years to get him to understand. She says she was insecure from the beginning of the marriage because her father never loved her properly. She says she is entitled to have her needs met. Once her needs are met, she says, she will be happy or secure. That's her narrative.

The events may or may not be true, but the narrative *is what she believes*. It's the kind of story we tell ourselves about our lives, about who we are and how we got there. And with that story, we craft the house we live in. The roof might leak, there might not be furniture, but it's the house we built. Even if that house causes suffering, it's our house. The story that builds the house might not be true, but the worse we feel, the more we hunker down in that house we have created.

Think about your narrative and how it defines who you are. Are you a leader or a victim of your childhood? Perhaps you are a chronic caretaker or you see yourself as depressive or disabled or insecure or disordered in some other way. Is your unhappiness because of the person you are living with or working with, or is it caused by your upbringing or genetics? Will happiness come when you have enough money and love, and when your children are grown and secure, or do you believe it will never come? The answers to these questions are part of your narrative. These are the building blocks of your house.

But suppose what you think you need is not really what you need, and all of those explanations for your unhappiness are not accurate? What if the things you *think* will make you happy *won't* make you happy?

❧ ❧

One summer I taught a seminar for autobiography writers. I began the seminar by taking ten minutes and telling the story of my life. I talked about a childhood of loneliness, abuse. Moving on to the years of my marriage, I told about my wife's cancer and subsequent MS, about our children, about quadriplegia— and I described my current sense of joy and gratitude. And then I asked this group of writers why I had chosen to tell my life story *that way.*

"There could be a hundred different ways to tell my life story," I said. And I had chosen just one.

After that, I invited each person in the group to write a five-page autobiography. When they were done, we talked about it, and I asked them to question why they wrote that particular story first, what the message was they were trying to convey, and whom they were actually speaking to. Then I had them go back and write a different story. We did that three times—until they got frustrated.

Then it was time to take a different approach. This time, I told them to write five pages of description.

"I want you to tell me who you are—without telling me how you got there or what it means."

At the end of that assignment, people seemed more invigorated and the room felt safer and more intimate. They were more comfortable being vulnerable—being known. I told them the only truth we really know for sure. All we know is *how we experience our lives*. The rest is conjecture.

When we release our grasp on our narrative, we find ourselves in exactly the same place as Jake when he stood on the floor, alone, reaching out, not knowing what would happen the very next moment. In other words, very, very scared—and then, with one small step, our lives open to a whole new future.

RELIGIOUS PERSPECTIVES
OF A THREE-YEAR-OLD

Jacob and I have been seeing each other on a regular basis since he was born, so I can remember what it was like for him (and for me) as he became aware of the world around him. Like most small children, he was filled with awe and delight. Sometimes when we were playing in my driveway, he would stop what he was doing and point silently to the sky. Five seconds later, I would hear an airplane. And I realized it was not just that his *hearing* was better than mine—his *listening* was better. He was not lost in his thoughts about his schedule for the day, or what to do for dinner, or various other mental activities that can hijack a person's ability to experience their lives.

We know how children live in the moment, and despite the

fact that it sometimes gets on our nerves, they have something to teach us—something we have forgotten.

One day when Jacob was about two years old, he ran into my office to play with me. He climbed up on the chair and pointed out the window to a statue of the Buddha I have on my lawn. He looked from the statue to me and babbled something. Since he was just learning language, I said, "Jacob, that's Buddha." I watched as he seemed to take in my words. Then he repeated, "Doodie."

"No, no, honey," I said. And I carefully repeated, "*Booo*-Dah."

To which he responded, "Dooo-Dee."

Aside from the fact that he just turned "the awakened one" into a pile of poop, I thought he might be onto something. So I decided to accept Jacob's view of the world. I began using the name that Jacob had given it. Doodism. I figured that in the Doodist religion our houses of worship are parks and playgrounds. (We have no membership dues or building funds, and no baskets are passed around during the service.) Our prayers are about noticing—noticing the color of the sky as it changes during a sunset, or actually tasting our food during a meal. When Jacob and I are together, I try to listen better, so I can hear the airplanes before I see them. And the cornerstone of Doodism is that prayer and play are the same thing.

❀   ❀

About a year after the founding of Doodism, I was preparing to go away on a silent retreat that would last five days. I had to attend to numerous details before I could leave. Some appointments with patients would have to be canceled or postponed. E-mail messages would be left to stack up while I was away. I would not be able to respond to questions and issues posted on my website. The producer of my radio show would have to wait until I got back before we could confer about the next show.

And then, just a few days before my departure, disaster struck. During a huge windstorm a tree fell on the garage, crushing the roof. (Fortunately, my van was not parked inside at the time.) With all the damage that had been done to the house, I knew I would have to deal (once again) with the insurance company and contractors.

So—*why* was I going on this retreat? What could happen there that could possibly outweigh all the responsibilities that I would be leaving behind and the challenges I would face upon my return?

It was Jacob who reminded me. When I told him that I would be away for a few days, he asked if I was going on vacation and if he could come. I said it wasn't really a vacation. Then he asked if it was work, and I said it wasn't really work either.

How could I explain it in terms he would understand? I thought for a minute and said, "It's kind of like school. I'm going to learn stuff."

That's what I said, but I was thinking, *What I really am going to learn is to deepen my ability to experience my internal and external life with stillness and compassion.* But then I thought, How would I explain myself if he pressed me and asked what I was going to learn? What would I say then?

I guess I would say that I was going to learn to *sit and do nothing*.

And the more I thought of myself trying to explain that, the more I realized that I was going on this retreat to learn to do what Jacob does every minute of every day. It was what he had taught me to do in the driveway, in the playground, in our walks together when he would hear the airplanes that I couldn't even see, and when he paid attention to so much that was escaping my notice. I realized, on this retreat, I would be doing my best to relearn what he had already taught me once—lessons I would probably have to learn and relearn time and again. The wisdom of Doodism.

Jacob Rice, my teacher.

LOVE AND ITS INHIBITORS

A while ago I was having a conversation with a friend who is a geneticist. He mentioned a phenomenon in cell activity that I think explains everything about the opening and closing of our emotional hearts.

The scientific description goes something like this. In each of our cells are the genes that will express themselves in various ways throughout our lives. The color of your hair and your eyes, for example, are forms of genetic expression. These are evident soon after birth. Other genetic expressions occur later in life. But these "expressions" may not emerge right away. For a period of time (which could be many years), some genetic expressions are suppressed by what scientists call "negative control." Before the genes can express themselves, negative control must be lifted.

How does this happen?

As gene research has progressed—my friend explained—it has shown that we have what are called "repressor protein" molecules that sit on a region of the gene and block that gene from performing its function. Think of a childproof seal on the top of an aspirin bottle or the brake of a car, and you have the idea. Until the seal (the repressor protein) is removed from the top of the bottle, there's no way the aspirin can be released. Typically this repressor protein inhibits potentially destructive genes like cancer genes. Typically this protein works well for us. Typically.

❀ ❀

When I was a young child, I wanted to connect with everybody. And I saw goodness in everybody—not just my immediate and extended family but also the larger community. I really liked people and believed they were basically good and trustworthy. Then along came the adults (the first was my mother, then many others) who called me naïve. The inhibitors. I still had the full potential to love, to trust, to feel compassion—I still had all that love of life I was born with, but I began to feel something was wrong with my outlook and perhaps I really was naïve. I was confused. Because I still felt people were good, but my propensity for trust was now inhibited.

(Let me pause here to say, in fairness to my family of origin, these were first-generation immigrants. My grandparents had escaped the pogroms in Russia; what they learned there was that too much trust could get you killed. It may have been true for them, and so they learned to inhibit those emotions. All parents pass their narrative on to their children who often absorb it—and so my grandparents' outlook had been passed along to my mother.)

Isn't this what happens to so many toddlers? They naturally express what they feel inside—emotions like trust, love, and faith. They have generosity: they want to help others. The world around them may become an inhibitor.

As Jacob reaches the age of five, he experiences joy in every moment, but the world around him now demands that his life be more structured, that he stop playing at certain times and lean into the future. Although this is necessary, what happens to that ability to experience *all* in every moment? Drop into anyone's mind at any moment and they are either thinking about the future or ruminating about some past experience. But rarely is an adult's mind doing what Jacob's does.

When will things begin to change for Jacob?

I remember when my grandson Sam was three years old, and he and I would take walks together. At that age Sam would tell me wonderful tales about the ants going in and out of the "mountain." Here we are, ten years later, and Sam is still able to experience his life like most kids his age. But he also spends a good deal of time thinking about his schedule for the future or how his friends might react to something he might say or do. Sadly, most children, by the time they hit adolescence, are already leaning into the future and living a life too busy to reconnect with the wisdom within.

Nevertheless, none of these inhibitory processes changes the potentiality that's in all of us; it's all *in there*, just waiting to be expressed.

✿   ✿

How do we remove the inhibitors?

First, I think we need to identify what they are. I can recognize the one I first encountered—the label, or accusation, or categorization of being naïve. To this day, if someone calls me naïve (which usually happens only when I talk about social issues and the healing process!) I can still feel the anger of a criticized child. (But today, I don't feel there is something wrong with my thinking.) Such labels are free-floating in our society. Are we called soft? Or gullible? What about too trusting? Or too emotional? Or what about too sensitive?

To be fair, some of the people who label us do so out of honest concern. Many of the people I treat are just like me, people I call tenderhearted. And there is good news and bad news about having a tender heart: we are more likely to experience our emotions fully, to feel compassion for others, to be more trusting, and to love more easily. On the other hand, we are more at risk for depression, anxiety, and mood instability. Without some inhibitory skills, we can be less resilient than others or be at risk of getting into unhealthy relationships. So it is understandable how people who love us would want us to have more protection for our tender hearts. But the problem is that when we hear these judgments enough, when we begin to think there is something wrong with us, then we begin to judge ourselves harshly. And then we feel we are not worthy until we get repaired.

Sure, if we are more naïve, tenderhearted, and sensitive, not only are we at risk of being labeled but we're also at risk of being hurt. On the other hand, I have grown to realize, after being hurt many times, that I can survive it. I don't like it much, but I also know that it doesn't last. So now my heart is open more than it is closed, only because I am much less afraid of being hurt.

But what about the opposite—the word, deed, or expression that removes the repressor and allows the release of the wisdom that we carry within us? In microbiology we have discovered that the release is provided by a small molecule called an inducer. The inducer binds to the repressor, and the paired complex is removed, allowing the gene to express itself.

So—what exists in our world that can act as an inducer?

It could be someone who comes into our lives and stays with us through adversity. That "someone" is a person who has faith in the wisdom within and has the courage to simply be with us through this difficulty—who doesn't feel a need to be "helpful" and offer advice but trusts that just being present is all the help we need. It could be almost anyone who approaches us with a curious mind and an open heart. *Their* empathy and their compassion are the small molecules, the inducers, that unlock the repressors. And as that happens—as we lose our judgments about our naïveté, our softness, our sensitivity, our trust, our compassion—we become comfortable taking ownership of what has always been within us. It's as if our genes were free, at last, to express themselves. And with practice, the expression of love and kindness will also take the form of *self*-compassion for the person we are, as well as compassion for those we interact with.

That expression is one of openhearted, genuine care for self and others. It is an expression of joy and love. It is something that nurtures ourselves and the world around us. Just like Jacob.

ABOUT DREAMING

I was a psychology student in the 1960s and, like all psychology students back then (I don't know if this still holds true), I was assigned to read Freud's *Interpretation of Dreams*.

To be honest it didn't make me all warm and fuzzy inside. Actually, it made me more sleepy inside. It was the same with Jungian and Gestalt therapy involving dreams. I remember talking to one patient about his dreams and thinking, *What the hell am I doing? I don't have a clue what this means and whether it's relevant.*

Granted, some dreams are prophetic. I've had them myself (and written about them elsewhere). That's *not* what this chapter is about.

I started thinking about a different kind of dream about thirty years ago, after my accident, when all my dreams were ripped from my grasp. Once I got through my depression, I could see more clearly. (By then I was in my forties, and seeing clearly meant wearing glasses and then bifocals. But I digress.) Anyway, in hindsight I was beginning to dream new dreams.

I thought back to my childhood when I was about ten years old, playing basketball by myself in the driveway. Some handyman (not my father—he was an anti-handyman) had thoughtfully put up a basket over the garage door, so pint-size Danny could shoot to his heart's content without being seen. I spent many hours shooting hoops . . . and dreaming.

That was the mid-1950s, when we were in the middle of the Cold War, back in the bad old days when we used to practice hiding under our desks during air-raid drills. I'd heard a lot about tension in the world, and I had a dream of becoming a world healer (yes, *healer,* not *leader*). I would be the one to bring countries together, get them to put aside their warheads, and work together for the betterment of all human beings. That was dream number one. But I also had another dream. I loved to make people laugh. So in dream number two, I became an immensely popular comedian. (Actually, there was also a dream number three. If I became a world healer *or* if I became a stand-up comedian, I would get to go on the *Johnny Carson Show* . . . which was my *ultimate* dream.)

Decades later, as a forty-year-old who was quadriplegic, I reflected back on those dreams I'd had shooting hoops. I saw that both of my serious dreams had something in common—caring for people, helping people feel safe and maybe even happy. That dream never went away.

All children have dreams. Jacob was three years old when he told me his dream of being a fireman. At four, he dreamed of being a railroad conductor. Maturing to the age of five, he settled on the dream of being a pirate—specifically, "Jake the Pirate."

I forget what my grandson Sam dreamed at that age, but as I write he has reached the age of thirteen, when his love for baseball overshadows all else. That love has strengthened and deepened—and so has his skill—as he has progressed to more advanced teams and has won accolades for his performance on the field. Now his dream is to be a *major league* baseball player.

A friend's daughter, twenty-two and a college graduate, dreams of becoming a makeup artist to Broadway stars.

Three very different young people, at very different ages—and all have their dreams.

But most of my patients are thirty-five and older, and when I ask them what their dreams are, they say either they don't know or they don't have any. Many men tell me they don't even have time to dream. That saddens me.

Dreams open our hearts and minds to possibilities. Dreams are what happen when we're on a playground. My first playground was my driveway. Now my playgrounds involve watching the ocean or almost anything nature has to offer. Playgrounds happen when there are no deadlines or expectations. They happen when we have nothing to do. (And the same with children, by the way. Children can be creative only when they are on their own, even when they're bored. That's why these overscheduled children worry me. They will learn lots of information and even develop lots of skills, but I fear they might not have time to dream.)

So, at any age, everyone has to go to the playground to maintain mental and spiritual health. What saddens me is that so many people don't go to the playground.

There are some things dreams are *not*. They are not five-year plans. They're not things we grasp onto, declaring the only possible way to be happy is by realizing them. Because if we're unhappy along that road, by the time we reach those dreams our brains are already trained for *un*happiness. Dreams are not wishing for what you had yesterday. They are not wishing for other people to change. They're not even the wish to lose ten pounds or to make more money. That's desire. And as you look back over your life, I'm sure you can see that desire can be a gift and a curse. It cuts both ways.

Dreams are visions and wishes—of what our hearts long to be, to say, to contribute to the world. Having a dream means having a vision of a life in which we can go to sleep at night and say, "How blessed I am to be living this life!"

Dreams happen when your heart is open, and cannot happen when your mind is closed. Dreams are about the heart's calling to find itself.

❧ ❧

A number of years ago I read a book by Stanley D. Klein and Kim Schive—*You Will Dream New Dreams*—for parents of children with autism spectrum disorders. All parents have dreams for their children that are dashed when they discover that their children have disabilities. Because of the healing spirit in all of us, parents dream new dreams.

It's no different for the rest of us. After Jacob gives up his dream of being just any pirate, perhaps he'll dream of being

Blackbeard. It's unlikely Sam will dream of being a major league ballplayer a few years from now—but who knows?

I am living my dream right now, but with my age and body, I want to cut back a bit, and I have faith I'll dream new dreams. Looking ahead, I just want to spend more time in the playground and see what happens.

PART 2

✳

Our Stories and Our Selves

THE MOST IMPORTANT
RELATIONSHIP IN YOUR LIFE

Often, clients talk first about relationships. The problem, they will say, is how they get along with a parent, a spouse, or children. They talk about conflicts, hurt feelings, misunderstandings—about relationships that seem to be falling apart or beyond repair. A frequent complaint is that they don't feel understood and that when they open up, they feel judged rather than supported. I've heard this complaint from patients, friends, and family members almost daily for my entire adult life.

In my younger days, I felt that myself. I spent many years feeling the great pain of not being understood. Like many children, I've heard the phrase, "Oh Danny, I know you better than you know yourself!" With that, I would feel the anger, resentment, self-pity, and ultimately the anguish of feeling alone in the world—all of which was made worse after my accident, when people were telling me how I *should* feel, how I *would* feel, and what I *could do* to feel differently.

So many people feel alone because they tell themselves there is something wrong with them that needs to be fixed. But of course that's not true.

These days, when a friend tries to fix things for me, I find I can joke about it. My friend might say, spontaneously, "Aren't you cold? Don't you want a sweater?" and we laugh when I respond, "Now that you mention it, I *am* cold. You always seem to know what I want!" (Of course I say that whether I am cold or not.)

But why can I laugh about that now when, years ago, it used to enrage and depress me? I had been living in that dark and lonely place for many years when I realized what had been true all along: I really was alone, *I* wasn't even connected with *me*. For all those years I had ignored the person I was and had just focused on my problems or other people's problems or whatever was going on. Until, finally—and I don't remember when it happened—at some point I misplaced Dan. So whenever I encounter someone who says they feel alone in the world, my question is, "What's your relationship like with *you*?"

Often people look at me as though I have just said something in a foreign language. Inevitably their first reply is, "Gee, I never thought about that." But when I ask them to take a few minutes and think about it, I have never heard them say that it's a good relationship.

So then I ask them . . . *How would you like to spend the rest of your life with the person you are right now?* The person who tries to do the right thing and who fails more than they want to? The person who might be overweight or underexercised or has a mean streak or a bad temper? The person who feels not good enough or unworthy of love?

Most people, when asked how they would feel about spending the rest of their lives with the person they are, say that's not a pleasant thought.

I find that heartbreaking. Because we really have no choice.

❧ ❧

How can we get along better with ourselves? Most of us have internal critics that tell us that if we were better people, then we would be okay. If we could become our idealized selves, then we would be lovable. So whenever we become aware of an imperfection, we kick ourselves in the butt repeatedly, somehow thinking that will make us better people. (No wonder dogs sometimes look at us like we're crazy.)

That intervention (kicking ourselves in the butt) doesn't work so well. Even so, it hasn't stopped most of us from judging ourselves even more harshly. I've had people in therapy who criticize themselves because they are criticizing themselves! (Our ability to be creative in our neuroses has always been so interesting to me.) But, realistically, what else can we do?

Let's try a different approach to work out this relationship. When I ask people what they would like from any intimate relationship, most say something about wanting someone who loves them for who they are, warts and all. They want someone who won't judge them harshly, who really understands them and wishes for their well-being. Now that *would* be a wonderful relationship. Someone like that would be the perfect mother, father, lover, friend.

You probably see where I'm going with this . . . so, do you think there's any chance you could do that for yourself?

Could you love that person in the mirror, warts and all? Even if you couldn't love that person quite yet, do you think you could feel kindness and compassion toward him or her?

Most of us are nowhere near there. We are so busy chasing after some unfulfilled wish, or running away from an invisible nightmare, we really don't take much time to get to know the person in the mirror.

Attaining this begins with doing nothing.

I know, I know . . . *who has time to do nothing*? I can hear you saying, "Even if I did have time, I don't have the luxury to do that because there is so much that needs to be done."

The truth is, most of our behavior is habit. A racing mind, running on adrenaline, is in a groove where it keeps on racing. Even our worldview is a habitual pattern. So doing-something-we-always-do feels normal, even if it doesn't feel good. Our brain/ body resists doing something that feels different.

The only way to break habitual patterns is to begin to do things that do feel different—maybe even a little uncomfortable at first.

❦ ❦

To get a sense of what doing nothing is really like, let's take a situation I'm sure everyone is familiar with—getting stuck in traffic. You can't move forward, you can't move back. You are literally stuck in your life, powerless to do anything. Most people get angry or frustrated, worried that they won't get to the appointment on time or that the car will run out of gas or their bladder will run out of capacity. One common definition of stress is the desire to make the moment you are in different. Since that's impossible, you sit with all of these uncomfortable emotions and a racing mind.

Of course, given technology, you rarely have to face the present reality without distraction. Get on the cell phone and make some calls. Answer e-mails. Update your appointments and your to-do list. There are so many ways you can distract yourself. News, music, audiobook, e-book, paperback, or magazine. If you are well enough equipped and sufficiently prepared, your time stuck in that traffic jam might even be said to pass quickly.

But what if you came unprepared? What if you are really just stuck there, for an indeterminate amount of time, moving neither forward nor back, dealing with whatever thoughts and feelings you have? What if you really have no companion other than yourself?

This is a situation that most of us, I think, find hard to tolerate. It's when we have no choice but to sit with ourselves.

❧ ❧

One client I worked with several years ago, Phillip, had grown up with two overbearing parents who divorced when he was seven years old. His way of coping with their intrusiveness was to shut down and become very passive. Now Phillip was married to a woman who had severe posttraumatic stress disorder and was quick to become angry or tearful. Their eight-year-old son and twelve-year-old daughter were buffeted by their mother's moods. Phillip felt powerless, as he had as a child. He felt unable to protect his children. Trying to please his wife, he worked two jobs so that she could be a full-time mother and so they could send the children to private schools. When Phillip's wife was under stress, she would blame him for all the problems in the world. She became verbally and sometimes physically violent—a number of times in front of the children—screaming about his worthlessness and incompetence.

Because of Phillip's childhood experiences, he not only didn't know what to do, he was afraid to do anything. He talked about how his family was stressful and how his wife needed help, but he couldn't identify what he was feeling beyond "stressed" and "unhappy." He had been disconnected from his emotions and his body since childhood.

When he began therapy, he wanted to take up the issues of standing up to his wife, taking control of his family, and getting into marital therapy. Ultimately he wanted to come to a decision about whether to leave the marriage—and, if so, *how* and *when*.

Predictably, none of these decisive strategies worked. The issue, for Phillip, was not so much about the story. It was about Phillip himself. And it wasn't solely about his relationship with his wife or his parents as much as it was about his relationship with himself.

When I asked Phillip during one of our sessions how he experienced himself living inside his skin, he couldn't answer. I taught him some basic mindfulness techniques that began with simply observing his breath, and then we spent about twenty minutes just observing how his body experienced breathing. I asked him to identify where he felt his in-breath most clearly. Was it in his nostrils or chest or diaphragm? After he attended to the in-breath for a while, I asked him to focus his attention right at the top of his in-breath at the moment when he let go. And so on—all of this to help him simply experience his body and its subtle movements. It was the beginning of what I hoped would be a good relationship. And as we continued this guided practice, I invited him to notice how his thoughts often got in the way of his ability to attend to his breath and, without judgment or commentary, to gently bring his attention back to his breath. He did well with this exercise. I encouraged him to do this daily for a week and said we would talk about the results the next time we met.

When Phillip arrived the following week, he said that, through the practice, he had become aware that almost all of his thinking involved regretting the past and fearing the future. But how did he feel right now, at this moment? He couldn't really say. And he laughed (a laugh of recognition) when I told him about an Alcoholics Anonymous saying that a friend had told me about: "When you've got one leg in the past, and one in the future, you wind up peeing on today."

Would Phillip be willing to try living *today* in the present moment? What would happen if he were alone with himself, in silence? What if he could spend some time in all the busy traffic of his life, not looking forward or back, not expecting his angry wife to change her ways or his demanding bosses to give him a break? What if he were *all alone with Phillip*? What if he got to know the one person who—absolutely and irrevocably—he would have to live with all his life?

He began trying. The next thing I knew, there was an e-mail waiting for me from Phillip:

I didn't realize how hard it would be to keep my mind from either dwelling in the past or racing forward. I suppose the main reason is, I have been living that way for so long without even knowing it. I do have to admit that it does feel good for stretches at a time while I am going through it, to actually live in the moment and not be a victim of my own thoughts and anxiety. But a practice like this is completely foreign to me and will obviously take some getting used to.

Finally, I thought. Phillip had stopped raging at all the traffic and had begun to discover what it was like to be alone, by himself, *with* himself. And perhaps he would discover that when he could hold himself with compassion, he could hold others with that same feeling whether he agreed with them or not. And he will soon discover that when he can sit with all of his emotions and when he no longer fears them, he will no longer fear those emotions in others. While I didn't know if his marriage would stay together or not, I did know that if Phillip could find compassion for himself, he would be more likely to find well-being regardless of his decision. And that is freedom in the deepest sense.

THE STORIES WE TELL
OURSELVES AND EACH OTHER

A number of years ago, I had as a patient a beautiful young woman who was born in Ukraine and moved with her family to the United States when she was ten years old. Now in her late twenties, Dariya was radiant and full of life. She was brilliant (in my estimation), and she was doing very well professionally. She had just received her doctorate in genetics.

Dariya was also resilient. During all the time she was working toward her PhD, and even before, she had been coping with serious health conditions that grew worse while I was seeing her and that made navigating her demanding internship much more taxing. After many tests, she went to a neurosurgeon and learned the bad news. There was a small tumor on her spinal cord that might or might not be malignant. Surgery could solve the problem, but it could also sever some nerves.

Dariya was in dire straits and had to make a decision about this surgery. Moreover, she knew there was a good chance that if she had the surgery, she would become disabled. After months of agonizing and trying to function as a vibrant young woman with multiple adversities, she decided to go ahead with the medical procedure.

The surgery did not turn out as she had hoped. I have said we usually live between fear and wish. What happened to her was what she feared. During surgery, some nerves were severed, leading to loss of bladder function. After recovery, she looked fine on the outside. No one looking at her would imagine that this was a woman who was constantly dealing with bladder malfunction and other consequences of the surgery.

After the operation Dariya had to drop out of her postdoctoral studies, give up her apartment, and move back to her mother's home. The surgical procedure and the aftermath were costly, and her career suffered. Having been out of the house for ten years, Dariya had developed a life of her own, but when she returned to live with her parents, her mother preserved many of her ways from the "old country." Inevitably this set up another stressful scenario.

Dariya was fatigued. She didn't know what the future held for her.

But here's the thing: *I* was not worried about her. After all those months of seeing her in therapy, I felt I knew her. I knew about her ability to overcome adversity with resolve and grace.

And Dariya knew it, too. That ineffable "something" is there for almost every human. (But most of us don't know it and, if we do, don't trust it.) Despite her youth, without being able to verbalize it, Dariya knew there was something inside. And that "something" was like a boulder that settled at the bottom of the ocean and didn't move, regardless of what was going on up top. She couldn't feel it then because she was on top of the water, in a tsunami. But the boulder was there.

❧ ❧

Dariya put weight back on and she put her smile back on. She actually looked great on the outside, though she did not feel great on the inside. And she suffered terribly.

But people react to what they see, and what they could see was a beautiful woman with a radiant smile. What they did not see was the woman dealing daily with unseen medical issues. They could not see what she had gone through and what she went through almost all day long.

Dariya sometimes felt angry when people responded to her in a positive way, once commenting, "They're just responding to the shell, they have no idea who I really am or what I've been through." She wanted to be able to tell her story to everyone who mattered to her. And she tried. Almost compulsively, she told the details of what she had been through. But every time she tried to explain her life to someone, she would tell me, "They still don't get it." Consequently she would become angrier, feeling hopeless and alone. And she was afraid that was the way she would continue to feel for the rest of her life.

I too had experienced that feeling, and it was one of the most painful of my life. After my accident, people looked at me differently and spoke to me as though I were fragile. I was profoundly alone and desperately wanted people to know *what it was like to be me* so that I would feel less alone. But I didn't have words to describe my inner life. I only had words to tell my story. When I felt no one would ever understand me, I truly wondered about my own humanity.

So I helped Dariya understand her relentless compulsion to tell her story—that the compulsion is about our human calling to connect, to be understood and accepted for who we are at our core.

When something extraordinary happens to any of us—as it did to me—we have no guideposts, no role models. We feel profoundly alone. We are desperate to reconnect with our community, our loved ones, and—most of all—to reconnect with ourselves. What we want most of all is what we had yesterday.

As Dariya and I explored the intellectual question of why we need to tell our stories, I asked her to listen to her body. Was it her body that needed to tell the story? I understood from Dariya that if her story were not told—she felt deeply—she would be misunderstood, or not understood, for the rest of her life.

What she wanted, what I have learned that I want—what we all want, I believe—is for people to "get" our humanity. My story is a poorly designed vehicle, as is yours, because we can tell our own stories in so many different ways. And although many people cannot relate to a bladder problem or a spinal cord injury or sexual abuse, they can relate to the experience of our lives. However we tell our stories, the message about our humanity is the same: I want people to know my heart. That I am a kind person who always tries his best to do the right thing in life and often fails. That I am, furthermore, insecure and vulnerable and dependent and comfortable and independent. Yes, all these things. Just like you.

Sometimes I get into bed at night and I feel so vulnerable and alone that all I can do is put my hand on my heart and quietly weep. And sometimes my heart is so filled with love that all I want to do is nurture the world and rejoice in what's around me. My heart loves and fears. My heart aches and breaks and rebuilds and rejoices. My heart opens and closes and nurtures my body and my spirit, and it contains the wisdom of my life.

This is the essence of my story. And Dariya's. And yours.

WHEN LONELINESS TAKES YOUR BREATH AWAY

Carl Jung was probably the first to describe the archetypal child that lives inside all of us. Like Jacob, this is the child who instinctively responds to what is astonishing, wonderful, or mystical. Here is the child who feels awe, the child who has uninhibited experiences almost moment to moment. That child inside us is eager and curious, searching the world, encountering what is new, exploring what is mysterious.

And something else. This child inside each of us is unlike any other human being in the world. In our DNA we are almost exact duplicates of each other. But somewhere in our genetic make-up there are slight differences that distinguish us from our fellow human beings.

It would be glorious if we could truly celebrate and enjoy the things that differentiate us from all others. But unfortunately that's rarely what happens. Instead we search for kindred spirits because we all share a yearning to be accepted by the families, communities, and societies in which we live. At the core of being human is our wish to *belong*. After all, the human brain is really a social organ that thrives and develops based on interaction with its environment.

We are social animals. Without social connections we are at increased risk for depression, suicide, heart attack, stroke, and a range of other conditions that shorten our life expectancy. On the other hand, at the core of being human is the knowledge that we are unique—different from all other humans. This human dialectic can be a source of great suffering, or it can be a source of creativity and even well-being.

One of my patients is a forty-year-old woman, Reba, who grew up in conservative Lebanese society where the rules and expectations were clear and absolute. Women were second-class citizens, their destiny determined for them from the time they were born. She was taught implicitly and explicitly that a woman's role was to serve a man. Even as a very young girl, Reba was uncomfortable with these traditions. She observed her mother and three sisters being submissive, but their compliance felt wrong to her. As she grew into adolescence, her doubts grew stronger. She realized she was living in a society where girls were being molested and even raped, and no one talked about it. The one time she attempted to tell her parents about this, they blamed her for "dressing *that way*." Meanwhile, those "proper boys" were getting away with drinking beer publicly and doing almost whatever they wanted. Nevertheless, she felt that she should try to comply with her parents' wishes and ordinations, hoping that somehow she would be okay, knowing that she wouldn't. She was at odds with herself. Should she do what was expected or stand up for what she believed in?

Most people, when they are uncomfortable with the world they live in, feel as though there is something wrong with them, something that needs to be fixed. Ask almost any child who grows up in a family where there is a mental illness or severe marital conflict, and they will tell you that for years they thought that the behavior in their family was normal and their anxiety meant something was wrong with them. Reba felt that way. And yet, there was also a part of her that knew something in her culture was just not right.

When she was a teenager, her mother died suddenly. Now there was added stress for everyone in the family. When Reba's father wanted her to be in a traditional (arranged) marriage, she didn't have the heart to add more stress to his life by refusing. So she married a man who was chosen for her.

Soon after, she and her husband moved to the United States. Leaving a culture that had never felt right for her, she arrived in Palo Alto, California, with a husband she barely knew. Talk about culture shock! Predictably, she felt even more isolated and vulnerable.

Of course things got worse—she was living in a strange country, coping with a new language and a husband who left their tiny apartment every day to go to work, leaving her alone. When we are isolated and devoid of human contact, we are at risk for all sorts of emotional problems. She became depressed and resentful, filled with anger and self-pity. Without love in our lives, we begin to question whether we are lovable or even worthy of love; such was the case with Reba.

She was depressed. She was angry. Day to day, she fought with the feeling that there was something wrong with her. Inside was the child who had grown into a strong-willed, creative, passionate woman. But that child had been born into a world where she felt she didn't fit.

❧ ❧

Many of us have experienced this kind of isolation, a sense of not belonging anywhere. I still remember going to my twentieth high school reunion a few years after my accident. The kid who had walked side-by-side with classmates through the halls, competed with them on the playground, and won many dance contests was now a quadriplegic in a wheelchair. Going to that reunion, I met with people I had not seen since before my accident. I was petrified.

The experience turned out to be even worse than I could have imagined. I sat at a table that was two steps up from the dance floor and buffet table, with no way to get further access. A classmate did sit with me much of the evening, but my God, how I suffered. A few people came up to me and awkwardly said hello, but most didn't even look over to me. I felt ignored and so alone that I just wanted *something* to end this suffering. Anything! Yet I knew I couldn't leave, because if I did, I felt I would never come back to these reunions—and my high school relationships had been precious to me.

While all this was happening, the trained psychologist in me knew I was being ignored because my classmates were anxious and uncomfortable. But *knowing* that did not eliminate the excruciating pain. I couldn't feel my body, but I could feel physical pain in my heart. I was so filled with shame that all I wanted to do was hide—but I felt so conspicuous. The longer it lasted, the less I knew about where to go and what to say. My self-confidence was horrible to begin with, but now the last remnants just vanished. All my social skills went away.

I didn't hate my classmates for ignoring me. I wasn't angry with them. It was beyond that. My shame went so deep I didn't even have the strength, the courage, to be angry. I felt worthless. And crazy. And profoundly alone. It was the kind of loneliness that literally takes your breath away.

❧ ❧

We have all experienced it.

I have a newly divorced friend who decided she would celebrate her return to single status by hanging out with some of her friends from the past. All of those friends were married—but she didn't think that would make a big difference. She eagerly anticipated being with them again, enjoying each other's company as they had before.

The day after she met up with her friends, she said to me, "I ate way too much. I couldn't stop eating. I drank way too much. I just wanted to make myself feel better, and I made myself feel worse."

She wanted to cure the pain of being different.

How do we tolerate an emotion that can take our breath away? The emotion is so powerful, we feel that if it continues we could die. We do anything we can to avoid feeling that sense of being alone in the world. We race around our lives. We eat more, drink more. We get busy, we work, we cling, we push—we collapse into bed at night, sleep too little, and wake up and do it again the next day. We're terrified of being alone. And it's inevitable, and with us from birth to death.

Analyst Marion Woodman put it best when she described the "divine child" as "always an orphan." And so we are—all orphans. The Lebanese woman alone in her apartment in a foreign country, the man in a wheelchair with pain in his heart, my newly divorced friend with her friends—we all live in a global orphanage. And there are so many others in that orphanage. What about the spouse in her marriage who feels unknown and unloved? A child in school who is ostracized by her friends? A gay boy or girl in high school who doesn't feel safe coming out? Or any of us who have experienced a trauma of any kind? At that moment, and for many moments after that, we feel painfully alone. All we want to do is repair that terrible feeling. And it's not fixable. We can do everything in our power to avoid the terrible pain of solitude, but we can't fix orphanhood.

But I think we know that. The aloneness is not an illness that needs to be cured. It's not a pathology. It doesn't signal there's something wrong with you—that you've been rejected or judged. It just means you're human. And the child you were, and are, knows what it's like to be alone.

So what's the difference between the pain of loneliness and the fact of being alone? What's the difference between the shame of loneliness and the gift of solitude?

Being alone is a fact of life. *Loneliness* is when we fight against that and assume something is wrong when we feel it. Mark Twain once said, "The worst loneliness is not to be comfortable with yourself." Many of us are afraid to be alone because we fear having to face our demons.

The question is: When you *are* alone, who are you with? Are you with someone whom you judge harshly or someone you feel compassion toward? Are you with a person who is not good enough, a person who needs to do better in order to be loved? Are you with a person who is unworthy? Or are you with that divine child?

❧   ❧

Over the course of our work together, Reba was able to face her insecurity and differentness and not rail against it or feel like a victim. Slowly, her anger dissipated and she reconnected with the young Reba who knew the truth of her life, who loved freely and was curious about everything. Young Reba was creative, delighted, and joyful no matter what the previous day had been like for her. Young Reba knew the truth of her life.

I told Reba about a conversation I'd had when I bumped into the mother of a high school friend of mine. Lillian was ninety-four years old and used a walker, but her mind was clear and her eyes still sparkled. When I asked her how she was and what her life was like, she told me that although she had visitors, she spent most of her time by herself reading or watching television. But she was happy. And then she looked at me with a big smile and said, "You know, Danny, who would have imagined that at this stage in my life I would be comfortable inside my own skin? How lucky I am."

Indeed, Lil, how lucky.

WHAT'S ENOUGH?

I sometimes have lunch with an accomplished friend who is the highly successful CEO of a multinational corporation. As with most who have reached his level of achievement, Patrick is a well-organized man who plans carefully. He always seems to know what needs to be done, and once that's lined up, he recruits people who have the skills and resources to meet his goals.

Patrick has a bright, warm smile, and is very engaging. Though his company's headquarters are in New York City, our friendship is so important to both of us that we make a point of getting together several times a year. When we talk—no surprise here—his heart opens a bit. (And so does mine.)

At one of our lunches, we were talking about his job. Patrick reflected on the fact that he was about ten years from retirement age. He said he felt himself getting tired. I know that, more often than not, being tired is not always a statement about physical fatigue. Many times, it is synonymous with being spiritually malnourished.

Wondering what feeds his soul, I asked Patrick what his dream was.

At first, he talked about reducing his responsibilities in the corporation he served. He planned on retiring and serving on the board.

I said, "That's your *plan*. What's your *dream*?"

I got a look that I frequently get when I ask this question—a kind of dazed expression that says, "I'm in a neighborhood I've never been in, and I'm confused." Or, to put it somewhat differently, "What the f**k are you talking about? Who has *time* to dream?" Both reactions are instructive.

So I asked him what his dream had been when he was young. "I never had one. I had a plan."

Obviously he had been incredibly successful with his plan.

But what had become of the dream?

❧ ❧

One of the reasons Patrick and I feel so close is because of our similarities. Both of us felt very insecure as children and have shadows of that insecurity. While Patrick and I enjoyed early success despite our insecurities, we both felt that we were really not as competent as people thought we were.

Patrick's talents were in business and management. Through a series of coincidences, combined with his native talent, he got a very high-ranking job at a very young age. He was *too* young. He quickly realized that he was in over his head, and if he was going to succeed, he would have to fake it. That he did—hiding his fears and vulnerability from others and eventually from himself.

Successes continued, and Patrick's level of competence rose to meet the challenges of his new positions. But the insecurity continued because he still felt like he was faking it. And like most, he felt ashamed of his insecurity so he did everything he could to hide it.

❧ ❧

Shame is the experience of feeling exposed and judged harshly. It's about ourselves—not about *what we've done* but *who we are*. And it is one of the most painful emotions we can experience.

When I was writing for the *Philadelphia Inquirer*, I was severely criticized by my editor and associate editor for accidentally repeating a vignette I had included in an article several years earlier. I felt overwhelming shame.

What does the mind do with shame? It can go in a number of directions. One alternative is to withdraw and isolate ourselves. (When the *Inquirer* editors criticized me, my first instinct was to quit the newspaper.) Students who are ostracized or bullied tend to withdraw and isolate themselves. When that happens, the shame can turn to anger. At its extremes, we can act out aggressively and humiliate others. (And as we know from the behavior of mass murderers—it's partly about the shame of being rejected by co-workers, feeling inadequate over and over, and feeling powerless to do anything about it.) On a lesser scale, shame can turn into anger, where we blame everyone else for our suffering.

And there's one more thing we can do with our shame. We can hide it and pretend it's not there. We can put on a mask of competence, put on our armor, and proceed into the world. Of course, some of this is natural and healthy, because we cannot wallow in shame. But in the process of pretending it's not there, we bury it more deeply.

But all buried feelings are buried alive.

So Patrick is tired. He has had big jobs. He has worked very hard on the outside, but over the thirty years of his career, he has worn a thick coat of armor and a mask. Sometimes he looks in the mirror and wonders whether it's himself that he is seeing. And Patrick, like so many others, tells himself, "If I finally achieve X, then I'll be Y." In that formula, "Y" means he'll be okay.

Yet there's a quiet truth in this good man. And in the quiet truth, he knows that when X turns to Y, then he'll have to reach Z, and then he'll have to start all over again. That quiet truth inside is telling him he is exhausted. But *change* is terrifying. It involves letting go. And if the only thing we have faith in is our accomplishments, how do we let go?

❀ ❀

After a long discussion, I asked Patrick *again* what his dream was.

"Dan, I never really had time to think about it."

I said, "Patrick, we have all the time in the world right now. Let's sit quietly in the playground of our hearts and souls and drink coffee and dream."

After a few minutes of silence, Patrick said, "My dream is to have something I've never had—*enough.*"

That's what we all want. That we *have enough.* And, more important, that we *are enough.* And we can only get there one very scary way—we have to expose our vulnerability and our shame.

In my own case—when I felt so much shame about the

mistake I had made in a widely read newspaper—I began to catastrophize and wonder if my horrible memory was so bad that I couldn't function. What could I do about it? The following week I submitted my next article to the paper. In the article I talked about what happened and the great shame and humiliation I felt. I talked about how a simple public criticism caused so much pain in a man who considered himself a very insecure writer. I went public with my shame, and the more I wrote, the better I felt. Within hours of submitting it, I got a phone call from my editor saying she had no idea that her words hurt me so badly and she was so very sorry. She said this incident was instructive to her and perhaps she should be more careful with her words and think twice next time before she pressed Send.

Shame is like mold. It grows in darkness. If I keep it inside, where it's moist and dark, shame grows. The only cure I know is exposure to sunlight. Not pointing a finger, but opening up to each other—one human to another. In intimate relationships we can expose our vulnerability, and the sunlight does its work.

We cannot experience love unless we feel known for who we are. And that doesn't happen until our vulnerable parts see the sunlight. When we feel loved, we can trust that we *are* loved for who we are and not for how we look or for what we do.

Then one day we wake up and realize that we *are enough*, no matter what. The "no matter what" is what is no longer hidden. And when we are enough, we can love and be loved.

ON THE PATH TO WELL-BEING

In nineteen classrooms of fourth- and fifth-graders in Vancouver, Canada, schoolchildren were given very interesting (nonacademic) extracurricular assignments. Some of the students were asked to make special visits, three times a week, to places of their own choosing—say, a mall, a park, or someone's house. Another group had different assignments: their tasks involved simple acts of kindness—giving a parent a hug, helping to vacuum the house, or sharing lunch with a fellow classmate. (Of course, the whole experiment was conducted with the prior consent of their parents and the children themselves.) The children's attitudes and behaviors were measured by researchers both before the experiment began and then four weeks later, after the kids in the two groups had completed their assignments.

The results? All the children who had the "kindness" assignments had a stronger sense of well-being and, in addition, were much more likely to be accepting of their peers. The acts of kindness, though unrelated to classroom activities, opened doors to establishing friendships. As noted by one of the psychologists who helped develop the experiment, assigning the adolescents to perform acts of kindness outside the classroom proved to be an avenue that could lead to a decrease in bullying and increased empathy and caring for others.[*]

Throughout our lives we are destined to make our own journeys in search of a sense of well-being. Many of us pursue wealth or fame or personal accomplishment, but once those are achieved, something always seems to be missing. The pursuit of happiness is a popular topic in the lay press these days. But once achieved, happiness can be fleeting. Or as one Buddhist author said, "After enlightenment, take out the trash."

Ultimately, we want well-being, a kind of wellness that begins deep inside. Those children in the Vancouver classrooms have perhaps discovered something about the search that they didn't know before—that acts of kindness are in a different category from the many other actions kids of that age are likely to perform. An act of kindness has greater influence than many other ordinary daily activities. As the study suggests—and as we know intuitively—the generous action actually alters the way we view others, interact with them, and regard them. And those who witness these acts also benefit from the exchange.

---

*Nancy Shute, "Random Acts of Kindness Can Make Kids More Popular," National Public Radio, *Shots*, December 27, 2012, http://www.plosone.org/article/info%3Adoi%2F10.1371%2Fjournal.pone.0051380

The researchers who conducted this study immediately began to think about its implications. Perhaps an increase in peer acceptance could benefit the classroom and social life. Maybe parents and teachers could "encourage these sorts of simple acts of kindness in children—or in themselves."

But I wonder what the experiment was like for the children involved in that study and how they will remember it later on. I think all of us have discovered that when we help others, we are rewarded with a sense of well-being that defies definition. Anyone who has volunteered to help a child or an older person or has read to a class of kids knows the feeling of "I got more than I gave." (I wrote in *Letters to Sam* how, shortly after my accident, my act of compassion for someone else—a nurse in the intensive care unit—changed my life.)

But as those kids (and all of us) get down to work in the classroom, in our jobs, or in our homes, the emphasis will be on *getting*, not *giving*. Getting better grades. Getting into the best university or getting the right job. Getting homes and clothes and cars and entertainment and vacations. Ultimately all of that "getting" is in service to finding security in our lives. And instinctively we believe that security comes with sufficient acquisition. But we are learning that that is not the case; once we have our basic needs met, acts of generosity actually increase our sense of well-being.

That's why we are hardwired for caring and kindness. There's a way in which we know that reaching out to others makes us feel good. We know that acts of generosity open us up to more relationships with our fellow humans. There's a reason all the great teachers in our history—from the Buddha to Jesus to Mother Teresa to some well-known Holocaust survivors—all teach that we should be generous of spirit and generous in deed. From the perspective of our evolutionary brain, it is only through care and cooperation that we have survived as a species. So our brains and spirits know about this.

But what happens to that knowledge? Does it go underground while we set about getting things done? Is it still accessible to us as we go on our lifelong search—the search that we all share—for a sense of well-being?

As the Vancouver schoolchildren get older and begin living their adult lives, I wonder how many will remember—either emotionally or intellectually—what they discovered about themselves when they were part of that very simple experiment. My guess is that it will be just as hard for them as it is for the rest of us, because as we move along the life cycle our focus tends to be more narrow and more about self and immediate family than about others. And of course that makes sense, because we must take care of ourselves and our families. But when life is in balance, we tend to be better off. Taking care of oneself to the exclusion of others leads to misery. Taking care of others to the exclusion of oneself is always a path to emotional malnourishment.

Most people who come to my office are struggling to be happier. They are in search of some sense of well-being that they may have never experienced but believe they can find on the outside.

But where is it? Those children in Vancouver felt a sense of well-being. When I was able to help that nurse in the intensive care unit, I experienced well-being, at least temporarily.

Well-being is a "felt sense." It's the feeling you have when you feel safe. It's a body's response to the belief that all is well in the world.

That feeling of well-being is inside of us. We have all experienced it somehow and somewhere, even if just for moments. But for many of us, it seems as though the sensation is lost or at least inaccessible.

And so we go on a mission-like search to find it again.

The Vancouver children got a taste of where well-being comes from, and with luck, that experiential memory may never leave them. But even if it does, they will always have the capacity for well-being, which only needs to be awakened.

I think the great yogic leader Shantideva got it right when he said:

Whatever joy there is in the world
Arises from wishing for others' happiness.
Whatever suffering there is in the world
Arises from wishing for your own happiness.

My formula is a fairly simple one: If you want more love in your life, love more people more fully. If you want more well-being in your life, reach out to others and offer them kindness.

Simple acts like this can awaken wisdom that may have been with us our whole lives.

PART 3

What Breaks Us

THE COMEDY LESSON

On March 2, 2011, I kept my appointment to give a lecture to a group of parents and staff at a residential facility for autistic children in suburban Philadelphia. In the annals of psychotherapy, this was not exactly an earthshaking event. As I try to do in all my lectures and on my radio show, whenever I give a talk or lecture I always have the context of the larger world in mind. I talk about the topic, of course—in this case issues around autism in the family. But then I talk about the relationship between parents and kids and how the quality of our relationships correlates with the quality of our lives. And then about the relationship we have with ourselves and how, if that relationship is good, everything becomes easier. And finally I talk about our relationship with our communities—strangers and the larger world.

I take it from the micro to the macro and back, always trying to demonstrate that we are part of the world and vice versa: despite what looks different, the core of our humanity is the same across communities and nations. I know I'm going to get some laughs, because I always infuse my lectures with a good deal of humor, in part to take a breather from what can be emotional material, but mostly because I have always enjoyed making people laugh. And there will be some tears, because I feel deeply that if hearts don't get touched during my presentation, minds don't get opened. And we've all had the experience of crying when our hearts get touched.

But the reason I remember this lecture so well is not because of its content or the reaction of the audience. For me the significance is that *I was there.* Six weeks before, that had not seemed possible.

❀ ❀

The story begins with one of the dreams I had when I was about ten years old, playing basketball by myself in my driveway. Working on my outside shot (which wasn't too bad at the time), I didn't dream of becoming a basketball star. (I must have known already it was impossible.) Instead, my fantasies took me in two other directions I have mentioned—the possibility of becoming a world healer or, alternatively, the incredibly alluring prospect of being a stand-up comic.

Fifty years go by. At age sixtysomething, I feel like I have spent many years trying to be a world healer, but don't feel I'm making a lot of progress. (I've done everything I can and the world is still pretty much in the toilet!) But there is that other alternative. The stand-up comic! True, I'm in a wheelchair, but I figure I can be a sit-down comic or a stand-up comic who sits down. (There are many variations on how I can describe my future stardom, but I will save them for when I am interviewed by *People* magazine.) So while I am musing about these things, my secretary mentions to me that there's a comedy club in town offering a monthlong intensive seminar in stand-up comedy. I figure this can only be a message directly from God, so I begin to make inquiries.

When I speak with the organizer, he assures me everything is wheelchair accessible, even the stage. He advises me to come prepared with a first monologue. When I ask how to go about that, he suggests, "Just think about the things that aggravate you—things that really piss you off."

As I think about his advice, I realize this is totally what I don't want to do. That's *not* how my mind works. After years of training and trauma and therapy and meditation, I tend to focus on everything in my life I am grateful for. I generally don't think about things that piss me off, and when I do, it takes me to a pretty dark and unpleasant place so I don't like to stay there. The more I think about my homework assignment, the more I get pissed off at that guy! So I am all set. That is to be the opening of my comedy routine.

I arrive at the comedy club on February 6th with a great sense of excitement. I also have anxiety—partly about the monologue but also about the mechanics. Will there be a place for my wheelchair in the rows of seating? How will I get up on stage? How will a guy in a wheelchair *look* on stage? And how about the fact that I am probably going to be a couple of decades older than anyone else there?

All this is going through my mind when I start down the aisle toward the stage.

A moment later, I am plummeting forward, flying through the air. I land facedown, my head banging against the concrete floor.

There are gasps, shrieks. I lie where I have fallen, facedown with blood all over the floor, screaming, "I can't breathe, please help me!"

❀ ❀

Much later, I would begin to decipher the details of what happened in that moment when I was flung from my wheelchair. But as I lay on the floor of the theater, I could not even begin to understand. All I could do was wait for help to arrive.

I was aware that my left arm, my dominant one, was completely paralyzed. I assumed that I had reinjured my spinal cord. I was able to tell people to turn me on my back while they were trying to immobilize my neck.

I was in severe shock. And shock is an amazing thing. I could tell people whom to notify, and I was able to tell the ambulance drivers which hospital had my records. And then everything went blank . . . .

❀ ❀

The injury was severe. I'd had a concussion. An MRI showed a blood clot in my brain. My spinal cord was indeed retraumatized, and I had injured all the brachial nerves from my neck down my left arm. That was my dominant arm, the one that I used to accelerate and brake in my van, hold a cup, feed myself, turn pages, hold someone's hand, and a thousand other things.

For the first forty-eight hours after the fall, because of the concussion I was confused and delirious. I wasn't quite sure where I was. I could not have said the date or the name of the president— what doctors ask to test your cognitive ability. Though there were things I wanted to say, I was not able to verbalize. For example, when

I wanted someone to straighten my arm out, I remember saying, "Cut my arm off," which is not what I wanted, but I couldn't find the right words. So I couldn't say what I needed, but I could cry.

The most dominant effect of the accident was the pain in both of my arms. The pain was so excruciating it felt like my arms were being stabbed with ice picks. I could scream in pain, and I did, much of the day and night. Finally my daughter Alison, a veterinary nurse, convinced the doctors to put me on intravenous morphine. Sadly, it didn't work.

I became septic as opportunistic infection raged through my weakened body. And as the nurses rushed me from my hospital room back to ICU, I could tell from the tone in their voices that I was close to death.

As my head began to clear and the confusion dissipated, I became fully aware of the magnitude of the disaster. My left arm, searing with pain, was paralyzed. That arm represented fifty percent of everything I needed to navigate through my world—and there it was, dead.

I recall saying to several people, *I am done now.* I had worked so hard, so long—and I was tired. I didn't want to do this anymore. I didn't want to go through rehab all over again. I truly felt that way. After all, I'd had great adversity over these last thirty years, and I also had received great gifts and had many adventures. I really felt that my life had been well lived and I was ready to be done with it.

And many people understood. After all, who could argue with me?

❀   ❀

I had a room at Jefferson Hospital that offered a view of nothing very special at all. From my hospital bed I could look at the window, but there wasn't much to see—just a gray and beige landscape of city buildings. A number of days after the accident, I was looking out that window at nothing particularly attractive, and for some reason I happened to look down at my dead arm. At the same moment—completely disconnected from what I was seeing—I thought about all the people who loved me. Who *really* loved me! Not just the ones who signed their letters "Love, Bill" or "Love, Jane"—but people who felt love for me. There were dozens of them. Perhaps many dozens. And, maybe for the first time, I felt all that love inside myself, inside my chest—and it felt warm and it felt big. It felt like it filled my whole chest cavity. My heart was beating faster, and I felt overwhelmed and moved to tears.

Then I thought of all the people I love—with a capital *L*. And there are many of them. And my chest got bigger and bigger and bigger. And I felt such groundedness, almost giddy with joy and gratitude. I felt my body almost couldn't contain all the love I was feeling.

And then, I looked down at my dead arm. And I said out loud to an empty room: "It's a fucking *arm*!"

I laughed at myself. Then I said it again. An *arm*. That's *all. And look at all the love you're surrounded with!*

❀   ❀

Of course, because I have a mind, and my mind darts and swerves, there was no chance I could stay in that moment. But I didn't forget it. The memory of feeling that moment was still with me when, a few days later, I was moved to Magee rehab center, a place I'd been many times before. Rehab began. My voice was weak and I could barely talk above a whisper. The pain remained almost unbearable. Though the arm had more movement, it was still not functional. But I was starting to look ahead at the possibility of living a life with pain and a dysfunctional left arm. (I wouldn't be aware of the effects of the concussion until weeks later.)

Needless to say, all appointments had been cleared from my schedule. I had planned to do a weekend workshop for autobiography writers in California one month hence, and that obviously had to be postponed. But with this constant internal experience of love, I began to reclaim my passion for helping people. So when the rehab staff asked me about my goal for rehab, I reminded myself of the lecture I was scheduled to give in suburban Philadelphia on March 2. I said I wanted to be able to do that.

Their response was that—whether we could achieve that or not (I don't believe they thought it was possible)—I should still work toward that goal.

And so rehab began the next day.

I was in speech therapy, trying to strengthen my diaphragm. (I couldn't say more than a sentence or two without taking a break for a few breaths.) Occupational therapy also occurred daily, as I had to find out what I could do with my partially paralyzed left arm and how I could utilize my right arm more. I had physical therapy in order to strengthen my slowly developing left arm. I also had to work on stamina and balance to achieve this goal.

On the medical front we were still trying to figure out what medications would be helpful in diminishing my relentless pain. Too much medication made me even more cloudy (I later found out that was one of the many effects of the concussion), and not enough medication left me with so much pain that I was exhausted by midday.

Nevertheless, I still worked on pursuing my goal.

I learned how I could put my lectures on my iPad and balance it on my lap. I practiced over and over trying to turn pages using my floppy right hand. I practiced my breathing and figured out how I could pause to catch my breath so my voice wouldn't fade away. I worked on picking up my adapted mug with my right hand (for the previous thirty years I had just used my left hand).

I still didn't know if the staff believed I could do it; but I believed it. I knew that March 2 lecture would be very different from any lecture I had ever given. But I knew I would be there, fully present and very grateful.

※　※

The day arrives. I am just barely mobile. I am going to make it to the lecture. But I have many, many fears. My voice still sounds very weak to me. Will the audience be able to hear me? I have pain in both arms. Will it become so intense that I have to stop in the middle?

I am anxious and insecure, but as predicted I am grateful and humble. And those are the emotions present when I tell the audience I am anxious and insecure. Then I tell them why. Not the whole story. It doesn't have all the details that I have included here. There would not be time, and besides, I want to talk about the subjects that I have come to speak about. So I just tell them about where I am and what this lecture means to me. I tell them about my right hand not being all that coordinated and I tell them I might have to pause frequently. And because I open my heart and show my vulnerability, the audience applauds as their way of saying they are with me. And so I feel safe, like I am with family, when I begin my lecture.

As usual, I speak about the micro—our children and what they mean to us. I talk about the difference between their diagnosis and their souls. And then I talk about the adults in the audience and the difference between their roles and titles and who they are at the core. We talk about relationships with others and our place in the world. Knowing that this presentation is going to be emotional for all of us, I begin by recalling the words I've seen recently on a bumper sticker, saying, "Mental illness is inherited. You get it from your kids." Of course the reason everyone laughs is because all parents know there is some truth in that. In the lightness of their laughter I feel as if we are all more connected. And, as I continue with my lecture, tears are shed. People feel me speaking to their deepest experience, with words that come directly from my own.

But this time I have something else to say to them, and it is connected to what I learned or experienced or felt or understood when I was alone in my room at Jefferson Hospital, my chest filled to exploding with the love I felt for other people and their love for me. And this is my conclusion: What if we could be lucky enough to look at our lives from a place of grace? What if we could see the things we anguish over, the things we are stuck on, and the things we think we desperately need that we are not getting? Suppose we could look down on our lives from that place of grace—where we are filled with love and gratitude. What if we could see our needs, our anguish, and our disappointments with a much wider and more loving lens?

And what if we could say to ourselves, "You know what? It's just a fucking *arm*. Look at the *love* I have in my life!"

COME HOME, YOUR BODY IS WAITING FOR YOU

Many months after my accident at the comedy club, I resembled someone who had processed the experience and recovered both emotionally and physically from the trauma. I say "resembled" because—as I would soon discover—I was doing a very good imitation of someone who had left that episode behind and moved on. Before long, I would see that this was not the case at all. But in the meantime, I was trying hard to get on with my life. I had resumed my weekly radio show. I was keeping appointments, seeing patients, giving lectures. All these things were done with difficulty as my concussion had a great impact on my ability to multitask and organize. So my clinical work was fine, but I was making more scheduling mistakes. My presence on the radio sounded good, but my production team had to help me in my preparation much more than previously. I wrote my lectures, but what had taken a few hours now took a whole day.

So my day-to-day routine was apparently restored to a semblance of what it had been before the accident, but there lingered some undeniable aftereffects. I had severe pain and some loss of mobility in my left arm as well as some unexplained tremors. I didn't drive as much. I had more difficulty integrating all the information a driver needs to hold on to. (This is information that we normally don't think about, but simply process automatically.) For example, I had trouble focusing on the car in front of me, the cars around me, the speed I was going, the bumps in the road, and the traffic lights. Given the difficulty of holding all that information in my head at the same time, naturally I felt more anxiety than ever going into new situations. I took extra precautions.

On the surface I seemed to have moved into a state of mind where I could look back on the experience without feeling overwhelmed. I was even able to joke about it. "My most important lesson from that day," I told people, "is that physical comedy doesn't work for quadriplegics."

Not a bad line. I really did feel as though I was moving past the experience I'd just had. My mood, I thought, was pretty good. But underneath the jokes and the coping and forgetting and the talk of moving on, Dan Gottlieb's body was not forgetting and would not forget. I just wasn't ready to listen.

❦ ❦

Among the things we know about trauma is that, afterward, most people go through a process of compartmentalization that is really self-preserving. It's almost as though the brain puts the visceral experience in a drawer in the memory bank. Unfortunately that drawer has no lock on it. So, later on, when we least expect it, the drawer opens and all those buried emotions revisit us (reinforcement of what I have said before: *buried emotions are always buried alive*).

Traumatic experience needs to be worked through. On a biological level, putting it in a drawer initially is healthy as it helps us recover in the short run. Eventually, we do have to integrate that experience so it gets released from that drawer and is no longer experienced as alien. But well-meaning mental health professionals have discovered that if we force this process to happen too soon, we can make things worse. If trauma victims go back to the disaster area too soon and reexperience the pain, the results are not therapeutic. We have learned a difficult lesson: opening the drawer *too soon* actually retraumatizes people.

What we need in the wake of trauma is support, some semblance of security, and a sense that we are not alone. We need to develop compensatory mechanisms to regain our stability and our strength—physically, emotionally, and spiritually.

What we cannot do is forget the trauma. Our bodies remember trauma—just as the body holds *all* the experience of our lives. But when do we listen to our bodies?

❦ ❦

When Gail first came to see me, it had nothing to do with any trauma that she knew about consciously. In the first sessions, when she came with her husband, the issues had to do with their marriage. They had been together for nearly twenty years and had two children. Gail's husband complained of a lack of physical or emotional intimacy. Gail was filled with fear, but that expressed itself as resentment. To her husband she seemed prickly and rejecting.

For a brief time I worked with them as a couple, and I could see the marriage improve. Both were able to communicate their hurts, fears, and desires more directly. And they were able to express their affection for each other more comfortably. Together they discovered what gave them joy, and they began to have more fun together. And both reported they were more comfortable when they left.

Six months later, I heard from Gail again. She asked if she could come back and see me—this time, by herself. She wasn't quite sure why, but felt she wanted to and needed to. Like many other tenderhearted people, she felt alone in the world. And she felt a disconnect from her family.

I was always interested in what she did with her body as she spoke. Her eyes would dart about the room—typical of someone who is anxious or distressed. During most of the session her shoulders were up, legs crossed, arms crossed. It was as though she was protecting her body from a potential danger. Most of all, her spoken language didn't seem to match her body language or her emotions. Sometimes when she was expressing her sense of alienation, she smiled. When I would ask her what it felt like to be in her body, she responded with words that told me she did not really have an answer. "Okay," she would say, or, "I feel tension in my shoulders." But she wasn't really aware of all the activity in her body. She couldn't say what her body was experiencing.

One day she began to talk about her middle-school experience. There was no change in her posture. With crossed arms and legs, eyes that roamed the room, she told me about how she had been the first girl among her classmates to develop breasts and how aware she had been that all the boys were talking about her. Then, one day, a group of older boys on the bus began touching her breasts. When she told her parents what had happened, they had done nothing to help her or support her. They seemed to shrug it off, saying, "Next time it happens, maybe you should tell your teacher."

Later on, Gail told the story of her first sexual experience in high school—how she had felt pressured into having sex before she wanted to. As with her experience on the bus, she had felt her body was being used by someone else.

Then Gail talked about her marriage to the "nice guy" I had met in our earlier sessions. She explained how she had married him because everyone had *expected* her to get married and, after all, "He was such a nice guy."

But she never felt safe with him. Now she wondered whether she wanted to be married at all.

With my encouragement she talked about the experience of being alone with her husband in the kitchen or bedroom. As she spoke of the sensations she felt when he was in the room with her, *now* she could identify what her body felt like. The closed, uncomfortable, scared, and angry feelings—all emotions her body had held since she was twelve years old—were in her neck, in her chest, in her pelvis, and in her heart. She was scared to death to uncross her arms, to feel the body of that young girl. She didn't want her breasts touched. "These are mine." She crossed her arms tightly as she cried, "I don't want anybody to touch them. Ever!"

And then new memories flowed in. She remembered the way her eighth-grade teacher stared at her breasts and the way her uncle touched her buttocks when he hugged her. She remembered that first boy who hadn't listened when she said she wasn't ready for sex, and how she felt so scared and violated.

Gail had become angry and bitter, like a porcupine protecting itself from harm. After all, at that point in her life she wasn't aware of how vulnerable she was and how violated she had been. So she was able to wrap her bitterness around herself like a threadbare coat in winter. It didn't really protect her, but it was all she had.

But her body/mind must have known that this was a safe place now. So the frightened, angry twelve-year-old girl began to open her heart. Gail began sobbing. It was as though her whole body was crying for itself. And I had a vision of her body saying, "Thank you. I've missed you. I've been waiting for you for many years. I need your care and compassion."

❧   ❧

The trauma does not go away. This I know. Yet I had been forgetful. As the months passed after my accident at the comedy club and I got into the role of "resilient Dan," I tried not to pay attention to the psychological symptoms from that trauma. The twitch in my left arm, for instance. The feelings of great fragility. My troubled sleep—and the way I so often felt tired in the morning. How could I not pay attention to all those signals my body was sending me?

What I couldn't acknowledge were the underlying emotions. When I practiced meditation every morning, I became aware of my mind constantly racing. When the mind races, there is *always* an underlying emotion. As is my practice, I allowed myself to feel that emotion fully. I felt the anxiety in my chest and was aware of how it radiated throughout my body.

The more I attended to the "felt sense" of my anxiety, the more my mind wanted to race away and ruminate about something meaningless. So I gently brought my attention back to my body and looked directly at this sensation I was calling anxiety. I know from many years' experience that when we stare directly at an emotion and just stay with it, it always changes. It might change in location, texture, or intensity. It might go away or it might even get worse. But it never stays the same.

As I stared at my anxiety and looked more deeply into the experience, the anxiety got worse and I felt terror. My mind wanted desperately to get away from what I was feeling. It's as though my mind was screaming, "Think about paying your bills, or your schedule, or what you're going to have for lunch!"

My heart was racing and my breathing was more shallow. But I stayed there. I couldn't abandon my body. But to come back to my body was excruciatingly painful and frightening. I felt so very vulnerable and out of control. I felt alone and broken.

Because I have grown to honor my body, I slowly became aware that I needed to attend to it. So I decided to sit in my meditation practice for a much longer period of time. And every time my mind began to race, I came back to the emotion over and over and over again until I was able to stay right where I was—frightened, panicked. I just allowed myself to experience the emotion and allowed my body to feel whatever it felt. So just when I thought I couldn't take it anymore, my body began to twitch almost like there was electricity in it. Thinking stopped. Feeling took over. My movements were so violent, I was almost afraid I could jerk myself out of my wheelchair. I felt almost out of control, but in a strange way I felt safe at the same time. (I wouldn't have been able to feel the intensity of these emotions if I didn't feel safe.)

So I put my hand on my heart and held that scared heart with a loving hand. I put my other hand on my face and caressed it as a caring parent would. And I began to cry. I cried for my vulnerability and I cried for how much I suffered in that moment. And when

I took a closer look at my mood, that terror gave way to sadness. That sadness gave way to kindness and self-compassion.

In a way, my body had been holding all that inside to protect me. Now it was calling me back. And even though I wanted to go away, escape it all, find some place far, far away, I was ready to return to my body, and stay.

❦　❦

There is, in all of us—in every human and in every living creature—the inborn desire to avoid what's painful. And when we experience pain, it usually gets resolved fairly quickly and we move on. But when we experience something this powerful and we try to turn our face away from our experience, it fails. The body remembers. Unfortunately, we remember our traumas, but we tend *not* to remember the fact that we have bounced back from every one of those traumas. When the body holds the suffering, we can't wake up to the fact that we are resilient, we are safe, and there is nothing to fear today. This is something we cannot know if we turn our backs on our somatic experience.

But if we can't avoid, forget, or deny, what are we to do?

Dr. Michael Baime is the director of the Penn Program for Mindfulness at the University of Pennsylvania. He was my first teacher about fifteen years ago and has become one of my dearest friends. When teaching an introductory course, he used a wonderful metaphor, reminding me of what a child does when splashing in the ocean for the first time. As the waves come rolling in, one impulse is to run away. But if you do that, the waves will knock you down. Another impulse is to stand there, be strong, and brace against the full force of the incoming wave. But if you do *that*, the waves will still knock you down.

The only way to maintain your stability is to dive into the wave. That's counterintuitive. The impulse to run and the impulse to stand firm are far stronger. But in order to get through trauma and get on with our lives, with our relationships, we have to do that counterintuitive thing. We need to take a deep breath and dive into the wave. And maybe, beneath the roaring foam and hurtling water, we will find the calm that lies beneath the surface.

OUT OF NOWHERE

Aviva, an eighteen-year-old freshman at Emory University, was in a restaurant in New Orleans celebrating New Year's Eve with some friends when suddenly she felt a crushing blow—as she described it, "like a bowling ball had been dropped from a rooftop on my back." She was hurled from her chair onto the floor, where she lay, hardly able to breathe, feeling the most intense pain she had ever experienced in her life. Though she didn't know it then, a stray bullet fired in the air from an automatic weapon five miles away had pierced her spleen and diaphragm and had become lodged in her stomach.

She survived the trip to the hospital, and as she was being wheeled in for surgery, asked one of the technicians, "Is it serious?" He patted her on the shoulder and replied, "We don't know.

We'll have to see." From that, Aviva surmised that her chances were about fifty-fifty.

Recovery was a long process. For more than a year afterward, this former athlete had to focus on rehabilitation of the most basic physical functions—eating, bathing, going to the bathroom, learning to walk. And that was just the beginning. "It was like walking through a dark tunnel," she recalls. "You are blindfolded, and you don't know the terrain."

This is what I call an out-of-nowhere experience. It is the experience I had when a wheel parted from an oncoming truck, soared into the air, and landed on the roof of my car. Where did that come from? Out of nowhere. It is my comedy club experience. It is the experience of a woman who is told that the lump in her breast has been diagnosed as malignant. Of a parent who is informed that their child has autism. Of a spouse who is told, "I want a divorce." I believe we have all had out-of-nowhere experiences, and, though the details may differ for each of us, we know what it feels like when all of a sudden the ground collapses beneath our feet and we are in freefall.

I tell people that all of the wisdom I've acquired in life has begun with two words: *"HOLY SHIT!"*

Then there are the other words that inevitably follow: *"This is a nightmare. It's awful. And it's not going to go away."*

The first time it happened, I told myself, "I can't live with this. I'll never be happy until I have what I had yesterday." And after a while, the "holy shit" was followed by, "Okay, what am I going to do now?"

What *do* you do when things come out of nowhere?

I don't think anyone really knows. Young or old, no one is really prepared. We silly humans tend to think we know what tomorrow will bring; this gives us a sense of comfort and security. But that's not the way life happens. Things catch us off guard, make us feel off-kilter, and change our course. Subsequently, we may label these things as good or bad. But while they're happening to us, we're like a rowboat buffeted by a stormy sea, and we feel frightened, helpless, and out of control.

So what can humans discover in those "holy shit" moments? When the stray bullet hits us, the truck tire falls down from the sky, and we are in freefall?

The content of Aviva's story and my story may differ from everybody else's, but I am sure that everyone has experienced at least one such moment. We know tomorrow is not necessarily going to be the same as today—we *know* that, and yet we still believe that, despite all evidence to the contrary, our lives are somehow predictable. And when we have our out-of-nowhere experience, we say things like, "Why me?"

❧ ❧

As I've mentioned, a lot of research has been done about post-traumatic stress disorder (PTSD) in an attempt to assess the impact of these kinds of events on our lives and psyches. For instance, many survivors of combat, most recently those who previously served in Iraq and Afghanistan and are now trying to adjust to civilian life, find they have wounds as deep and painful as any physical damage. Their symptoms, which may not show up at first, are now well recognized by mental health professionals. Sleeplessness and horrific nightmares. Explosive anger. Sudden panic in situations and terrifying flashbacks. Deep depression, often accompanied by addictive use of drugs and alcohol. Risky behavior, suicidal ideation—and, all too frequently, attempted or actual suicide.

Of course, these symptoms are not exclusively those of veterans. They can occur in anyone dealing with any kind of trauma—bereavement, illness, accidents, floods and earthquakes, sexual abuse, refugee experiences—the list is as varied as all the disasters that befall humankind. The trauma that comes out of nowhere may hit us as suddenly as a speeding car or as gradually as a slow-growing melanoma; it could be as irreversible as the death of a child or as irresolute as a trial separation. How we cope with life's surprises says a lot about how resilient we are and how much self-compassion we have. It also says a lot about where we've come from and who we were before all of this happened. But whatever the personal details, trauma involves pain and loss. And with that comes suffering, often with some, many, or all of the symptoms of PTSD.

But there is another aspect of trauma that psychologists call "posttraumatic growth." Richard G. Tedeschi and Lawrence Calhoun, two psychologists at the University of North Carolina at Charlotte, discovered that many people who struggled with the most severe kinds of trauma experienced many *positive* changes. "These changes include improved relationships, new possibilities for one's life, a greater appreciation for life, a greater sense of personal strength and spiritual development. . . . There appears to be a basic paradox apprehended by trauma survivors who report these aspects of posttraumatic growth: their losses have produced valuable gains."* Many people, myself included, experience both the chaos and suffering that go with trauma and the growth that can occur in its wake.

---

*Tedeschi, Richard G., and Lawrence Calhoun, "Posttraumatic Growth: A New Perspective on Psychotraumatology," *Psychiatric Times*, vol. 24, no. 4, April 1, 2004.

There is no twelve-step program leading to posttraumatic growth. It is, rather, the kind of long, dark tunnel that Aviva described. And we enter that tunnel blindfolded. As Tedeschi and Calhoun point out, trauma makes us feel more vulnerable, even helpless. It opens us up to unanswerable questions: Why did this happen to me? What is the point to my life, now that this trauma has occurred? Why should I continue to struggle? What can I believe in now? And it often confronts us with difficult truths—that some goals are no longer attainable, that we do not hold the place in the world that we thought we did.

But if we can make our way through that tunnel, we may grow in ways that we never could have anticipated.

The question is—where and when does that growth begin?

SHIVA HAPPENS

In Jewish tradition there is a ritual mourning period that takes place after the death of a family member. Shiva is a quiet time of sadness when we sit in a room and give ourselves over to whatever feelings we feel, whatever thoughts we have, for the person who has died. The community comes out and takes care of routine domestic tasks of feeding and cleaning. Friends and family offer constant companionship to the bereaved. Thus the bereaved has no responsibilities other than to attend to their own grief. It is essential to the ritual of exposing ourselves fully to feelings of loss and grieving for someone who was part of us. It's the process of opening up and saying good-bye. But it doesn't end with the week of shiva. The first week is part of another mourning period of thirty days when mourners are allowed to return to work but are asked to limit social engagements and festive outings. (It is believed that it is unhealthy to get up from shiva and resume a normal life.) And many families, after one year, have an unveiling, when the tombstone is finally put permanently in place and revealed to the community.

The rabbis who framed Jewish law and custom knew that grief was an ongoing process that didn't end at a designated time. They understood that grief came in waves of sadness that seemed to come out of nowhere.

When things come out of nowhere, when our lives are forever changed by events we cannot control, our first instinct is to try to bring back what we had yesterday. It's like the phantom pain associated with an amputated limb. It's as though the body/mind feels the pain where the limb used to be. But slowly, as we realize yesterday is gone forever, our heart opens, and—inevitably—tears flow and mourning begins.

All trauma involves loss. All loss is a kind of death. And all death must be mourned. Shiva happens.

In his book *Healing into Life and Death* Stephen Levine writes, "Grief is the rope burns left behind when what we have held to most dearly is pulled out of reach, beyond our grasp."* Unless we are lifetime Buddhists or meditators, we hold on to what we have; we don't let go of things easily. It's natural. How in the world can we let go of yesterday—of a limb that has been lost, of the ability to walk, of our image of being married and having

---

*Stephen Levine, *Healing into Life and Death* (New York: Random House, 2010), p. 102.

a family around us, of having a healthy body, of having a child who is near perfect?

How do we let go of the things that are so precious to us? And there are so many of those things. How do we let go of our image of a spouse who can really hear our hearts? How do we let go of our dream to have accomplished more than we have at this stage of our lives? Indeed, how do we let go of the psychological home we've lived in for all these years, despite the fact that it's too big, too cumbersome, has too many leaks in it—and yet it's our home! How do we let go of the threadbare coat that no longer keeps us warm but has been our companion for many years?

How do we *let go*?

A patient of mine recently said: "I feel like this life has been dropped on me like heavy snow on a butterfly. I have been fighting against this feeling for years. And now all I can do is cry and wait for the season to change."

If, as you are reading this, you are beginning to think about the losses you've experienced in your life and if you're beginning to feel sad or tearful, you've just found the answer. We let go through tears and sadness and fear and grief. But for most of us, tears don't happen until we let down, exhale, and open up to the truth of our lives.

❦ ❦

One of my patients was a forty-year-old woman who sometimes felt flooded with anxiety and had periodic bouts of depression. She told me about her childhood. She had been beaten by her mother between the ages of five and twelve, until she ran away and was placed in foster care. By the time she was seventeen, she had run away from foster care because she was being abused. Nevertheless, in the years since then, she had built a life for herself, found support in the community, made friends, graduated from high school, taken college courses, learned a trade, and found a job that turned into a career. Talk about heroic! But even though she was able to function, all the emotions she had felt as a girl were still there, but were buried, and so she couldn't form a healthy or intimate relationship.

But what of the emotions "buried alive"? One morning this woman felt a lump in her breast. It was diagnosed as cancer, and within a short time she had developed symptoms of PTSD. She started to mistrust her body and the world around her. In her words and behavior, she began to show signs of paranoia.

Over the course of several months, she began to feel safe in my office. In one session she began to talk and, moments later, she cried. Session after session after session, she cried and cried and cried. She cried for that girl who was scared and helpless; she cried for the adolescent who was molested; she cried for a lost childhood; she cried for the young woman who buttoned up and forced herself to go to work, who suffered. She cried for her body that was beaten and abused and now had cancer. And the more she cried, the more open she felt.

It turns out that the vast majority of people say they feel better after they've cried. Researchers have examined the chemistry of tears and have found that when we cry, our tears actually contain cortisol—the stress hormone. So crying actually diminishes stress. The deeper the wound, the deeper the pain, the greater the grief.

And what did I do? I held her. Not physically. I held her emotionally. She *felt* held. And this was her crying place. This was where she came to sit shiva for the thirty-five years of her life that were gone. And she sat shiva for a long time.

❀ ❀

After my mother died, my father and I became an important part of each other's lives. He and I spoke every day. We were father and son, of course, but also buddies. And later, when my father died, I literally felt an empty space in my heart, a hole that hurt so badly I wanted to turn my back on it. But I didn't, I couldn't. I kept washing it with tears. And every day it got washed out again and again.

This is sadness. This is how shiva happens. There's something about sadness that opens our hearts. And when our hearts are open, our lives become more open. We can accept the companionship and love of others. We can fathom a future. And then we can go on. We go on with scar tissue in our hearts, carrying memories of yesterday and the sadness of *what was*. But after all the tears, we are more awake to what is and what could be.

WHAT NOW?

It had been two weeks since my cousin Donald passed away, and I was having dinner with his wife Arlene. Understandably, Arlene was devastated and kept repeating, "I don't know how I can go on."

I remember thinking that was precisely right: without knowing how she would go on, she knew that she could. We *can* go on, and with very few exceptions, we do. We might feel as though we don't want to, but given the stark choice of life or death, we almost always choose life. When the unimaginable happens, when things come out of nowhere to change our lives, we have no way to see how our lives will be reshaped. There is no road map showing us the way, no light at the end of the tunnel. So the question becomes, "How *can* I go on?"

There is a Sufi saying that I have often quoted: "When the heart weeps for what it has lost, the soul rejoices for what it has found."

But I need to add, *"not right away."* Like the patient I described in the previous chapter, sometimes the heart needs to weep for a long, long time.

※ ※

In a discussion forum on the Christopher and Dana Reeve Foundation's website, I heard from a woman with quadriplegia who, in the eight years preceding her accident, had experienced a wide range of what she called "unfortunate events." She had been divorced from her husband, who subsequently attempted suicide. Her grandson had died of sudden infant death syndrome at the age of seven weeks, after which her daughter "spiraled down" with symptoms of bipolar disorder. In the years preceding the car accident that left this woman with a fractured spine, she had also experienced two home break-ins, four moves, and three job changes.

How did she survive such trauma? It changed the way she saw the world and how she saw herself fitting into the world. For the first years after her accident, spinal cord injury became the central feature of her life. Quadriplegia was not *what she had*, it became *who she was*. But then things began to change. This woman wrote about what she called "the takeaways from literally losing everything, including nearly losing my life." She listed those takeaways:

FAITH. I have learned that some things are not controllable.
   And now know I will be cared for regardless of
   where life's circumstances place me.
LIFE IS PRECIOUS. I say "I love you" much more frequently
   than before my accident.
KINDNESS OF OTHERS. My family and friends were treated

with unbelievable care and kindness by total
strangers.

PATIENCE. Waiting has become a way of life for me—
learning new ways to do things for my changed
and often uncooperative body.

COMPASSION. For others and myself, along with a deeper
understanding of how disabilities impact those
who have them.

FORGIVENESS. I don't believe most people awaken with
an intention to kill or injure other human beings.
Bad things happen in every human life.

So here was a woman who, after all her losses, could list what
she had gained. She was completely aware of how her life had been
damaged. Almost every day she felt overwhelmed and frightened,
longing for something she could never have. She experienced all
kinds of physical changes—the frustration and embarrassment of
bowel and bladder care, newfound dependency, and lost dreams.
Her losses were absolute. Justice had no role here. No human
being or deity would intercede to say, "You have given enough, you
have lost enough" or "Here are some victories to balance out your
defeats." But her mind had gone beyond that. Despite the many
losses, there were gains. The blows had come from nowhere. So,
too, did the takeaways.

❧ ❧

This is an example of posttraumatic growth. The trauma is not
really in the past. It is not forgotten. There are still those holes in the
heart—the damage that has been done. But in time, we cannot only
weep for what we have lost, the soul can rejoice for what it finds.
And we find ways to accommodate ourselves to the world around us.

I used to meditate by a lake every morning on my way to work. The lake was relatively small and beautiful, and I enjoyed looking at the water and watching the reflections of the trees. It was a perfect vision, as so much of nature is. Then one day I arrived at "my" lake to find that someone had thrown in a massive truck tire. The tire was highly visible, and in my eyes, it didn't belong there. I felt anger and a personal sense of violation: "How could someone desecrate nature like that?" But I also felt anger because this was what I would see when I was meditating. Something ugly. So, for the next couple of months, I would look at the tire and it would trigger the anger and critical judgment. But after a while, my anger dissipated. That tire simply became part of the picture. So, for a long time, I didn't pay much attention to it.

The following year, I noticed that the tire was completely covered in moss. It was as though while I had begun to accommodate the tire by not noticing it, the lake and the tire were accommodating each other. Now when I looked at it, it was no longer the tire in the lake. It was once again the lake. Slightly different, but basically what it had always been. We—the lake, I, nature—had found ways to accommodate.

That's what happens in our hearts. The holes do not disappear, but scar tissue grows and becomes part of who we are. The same takes place in nature. As the famous Spanish architect Antoni Gaudi observed, "There are no straight lines or sharp corners in nature." The most stable structures in nature—like trees or spiderwebs—have angular and curved lines. As our hearts grow larger, and we learn that scar tissue is not so ugly after all, we accommodate what we had thought would be unendurable. And we realize that the wisdom we have gained would not have been possible without the losses we have known, even those that seemed impossible to bear.

PART 4

✳

What Connects Us

MIRRORS

Some emotions are more complex than they appear.

After watching people express emotion in my office for more than forty years, I have come to believe that it is the experience of emotions that drives our lives. But the description or analysis of our emotions doesn't necessarily match the experience.

Emotions don't come with labels. People cry when they are not sad. They often cry when they feel something they hear or see "touches their heart." And when they cry they cannot describe the emotion they feel. They can't even say whether it is positive or negative, just "touching." Many people laugh when they are not happy: they may be nervous or angry, expressing hostile feelings with sarcastic laughter. What we call "anger" may actually be helplessness, disappointment, sadness, depression. And about the emotion called "happiness"? Once again let me ask: *What does that mean?* I felt happy at my daughter's wedding and my grandson's birth. Every time Jacob comes to visit or I hear a friend's voice, I feel happy. On the other hand, a pint of Ben and Jerry's Chunky Monkey ice cream makes me happy (that is, until it makes me miserable). But are they all the same? I've been thinking about this emotion for a couple of decades now and here I am, still clueless!

Sometimes, during a session, when someone is expressing anger or guilt or critical self-judgment, I am aware they are not present in the room but rather lost inside their habitual responses to some stimulus. And when that happens, I interrupt them and invite them to experience what's happening to them that very moment. When I am able to get them out of their head and into their body, they quickly notice that their heart is racing or their shoulders are tense or their stomach feels upset. They are suffering. If we are able to *stay present* with one another, and they are able to feel their suffering fully, they sometimes feel relieved or sad. Depending on where they are in their growth, they may even feel a sense of compassion for themselves.

All these things are happening to their body while their mind is engaged in habitual behavior. So the next time this happens (and there is always a next time and a time after that), I simply invite them to put their hand on their heart. Then I ask them to close their eyes. I see if they can feel the warmth of the hand on their chest, and perhaps they can experience that hand holding a tender heart that is suffering at that moment. Perhaps they *can* feel the hand that held a baby, comforted a crying child, embraced a lover. I invite them to feel the same thing toward their heart that they feel toward anyone or anything they love. And inevitably their bodies relax and often they begin to cry.

The emotions behind these tears may have no name, but there are deep feelings happening.

These are the feelings often accompanied by a big sigh, the feeling of "home." On a biological level it's the same feeling a mother might feel in a department store after her lost child is returned to her. The tears don't happen when she realizes the child is missing: the tears happen when the child returns, when the mother finally feels safe and can "let down." Tears happen when you feel safe enough to let go. Some would argue that this can all be explained by what is occurring in the nervous system. We begin crying, they would say, when the sympathetic nervous system (the one that activates a response) switches to the parasympathetic nervous system (often called "rest and digest"). But we know there is much more going on here. It's about a relationship that was momentarily pulled apart and then reconnected.

❧ ❧

We know that quality of life is all about relationships. The more we have, the more connected we are—the more love we feel coming from and going toward others—the happier we are. And the healthier we are. Psychologist Barbara Frederickson, in her book *Love 2.0,* explains that connecting with other humans in an intimate and loving way releases oxytocin, boosts our immune system, and even strengthens the vagus nerve (a nerve that connects the brain to the heart). So when we experience a connection in a loving relationship, it literally does our hearts good.

People who have recently experienced the breakup of a significant relationship are at great risk for physical and psychiatric disorders. As a matter fact, there is something called "broken heart syndrome" or "stress-induced cardiomyopathy": the weakening of the heart muscle by acute stress, such as death of a loved one.

Human relationships are so integral to our lives, as individuals and as a species, we actually have neurons that help us connect with one another. They are called mirror neurons. They fire when we share an experience with someone else. For example, if we witness an act of kindness, we experience a sensation in our bodies that we could rightly call kindness. If we are in the presence of someone who is anxious or depressed, we are likely to feel more anxious. That's why when we are in the presence of someone who feels that way, we try to help them fix their problems—so we can both feel better!

Many brain scientists say that the brain is a social organ. It is the mirror neurons that make it so. And it's not just intimate relationships that activate mirror neurons.

Watch a game where you see a basket made, a goal scored, a finish line crossed, or a run driven in, and as you become involved in the action, even at a distance, your heart will beat faster. If it's a sport you relate to, your muscles tense up in synch with participants out there on the court or field. You find yourself becoming a participant of some kind, even without moving a muscle. And if you are at a sporting event and your team wins, it feels like you are with thousands of "family."

As I write this chapter, the United States has just recently gone through the bombing at the Boston Marathon. And for the days and weeks after that, we were all Bostonians; we all felt vulnerable and frightened in the wake of the bombing. And we all felt relieved when the second bomber was caught. How does that happen when the events take place hundreds or thousands of miles away? How do we have that shared human experience? Thank your neurons for that. Inevitably, our minds and bodies get involved in lives outside our own. Something inside us reflects the experiences of others.

Scientists do not fully understand how this all works, but what they know for sure is that these mirror neurons are instrumental in creating relationships. (As a matter fact, there is some early evidence suggesting that people with autism spectrum disorders have difficulty with social encounters because there is a defect with their mirror neurons.)

Though there are mysteries about how mirror neurons initiate responses in our brains and bodies, we have plenty of evidence that they do. Note your response the next time you see a baby napping in someone's arms or smiling up into the face of a parent. The emotional pull is irresistible. You're not directly involved in the contact between parent and child; you're "just" an observer. And yet you're also much more than that. The love that you see expressed between mother and child, or father and child, resonates with a whole range of feelings inside you. Your mirror neurons have sprung into action.

And they're powerful. There are plenty of reports that new mothers begin to let down their milk when they hear the cry of someone else's hungry baby. So not only do those responses help us feel what others may be feeling, but they also help us grow and become more successful social beings. Things outside ourselves become part of our being and change us. We go to a movie that tells a happy love story and we are touched by the love portrayed by two actors. We get good feelings from a happy ending. Yet all we are actually doing is sitting in a theater. Thank those mirror neurons.

But didn't you always know you had this power? Since you were a child you have appreciated that someone else's smile makes you feel like smiling. Someone else's frown makes you sad, or concerned, or anxious. The sight of one person striking another creates a jolt in your own body, followed by a torrent of feelings ranging from fear to aggression. Catch sight of two lovers embracing, and your heart will be touched. Most of us have experienced responses like this ever since the day we were born and will continue to do so for the rest of our lives. That's just the way we're wired.

And the consequences?

What I do, or say, or express in front of you will change your very chemistry in ways that you and I cannot begin to control or understand. And the same will be true of your effect on me.

❧ ❧

So what happens when you and I are sitting across from one another, and I invite you to put your hand over your heart and feel kindness toward yourself? What happens when I look into your eyes and ask you to experience the kindness I feel toward you? You and I do not need to move from where we are sitting. We do not need to touch each other or to name our emotions. But something passes between us. Let neurologists call it neuronal activity or oxytocin. Let psychologists call it mirroring. Call it what you will. What I know is, we both are changed.

ABOUT CARING

Seven thousand five hundred years ago (as close as we can calculate), in a region of what is now the southern United States, a young boy with spina bifida lived to the age of fifteen. This would not have been possible unless he had constant attention from someone in his tribe or family. Today, with skilled surgery and the most advanced medical technology, a child born with spina bifida has a good chance of survival to that age and several decades beyond. Not so, seven millennia ago. This child, named the "Windover boy" by archeologists, must have received the most extraordinary kind of human care.

The tradition continues. We have a capacity for care that comes from millions of years of evolution. In the current tribe of humanity, we care for closest family members and complete strangers; for the guy in the wheelchair and the young kid in the classroom; for the pregnant mom and the aging aunt; for babies who are crying and those who are sleeping; for people who lag behind, trip and fall, get stuck or come unhinged. For all of them, and sometimes even for ourselves, we humans have reserves of something that we call "caring."

But what is it?

Several years ago while listening to the radio show *Fresh Air with Terry Gross*, I heard an interview with an anthropologist and a psychologist.

They had been studying a species of monkey in Africa, observing the way the mother monkeys responded to stress. To get a reading on this, they measured levels of cortisol (the stress hormone) in mother monkeys who had just lost their babies. They discovered that when a lion attacked the monkey colony, some of the mother monkeys who lost their babies recovered quite quickly (their cortisol levels declined). Others took much longer to recover (cortisol levels remained high). The mothers who recovered more quickly were the ones who were grooming *other* baby monkeys.

That's all about caring, which is the first step toward love. Associated with love, we've found, is another type of hormone I've mentioned, oxytocin, which is really the opposite of cortisol. Oxytocin is the hormone that gets released when your heart is open, your mind is open, and you feel safe. It's the hormone released when you fall in love (which is why we feel safe even though we're "falling").

But in my office, I don't see hormones, I see people who suffer. And when I encounter them with a curious mind and an open heart, they began to teach me about their lives. Many report that—for the first time in their lives—they feel as though someone is interested in their personhood. Not in their looks or their performance, their flaws or their symptoms, but interested in who they are.

❧ ❧

Many years ago I saw a woman who was highly accomplished yet feeling very alone and isolated. In our first session she said to me, "I feel like my soul is a prism but everyone I know only sees one color. Nobody sees the prism." That's not to suggest that no one in this woman's life cared about her, but it might suggest she hadn't experienced the kind of compassion that she longed for—that we all long for.

As I write, it has been thirty-three years since the accident I had when I was thirty-three years old. I've lived way beyond the expectations of doctors, friends, family—and myself. When I think of the incredible number of things that had to happen to keep me alive, I am humbled and grateful beyond all words, beyond anything I have felt in my life. I have been cared for. I have been the recipient of all this, and I don't even know why, or where it came from, or how it continues, or what it means.

And that has also meant caring for myself—as we all need to care for ourselves.

On that thirty-third anniversary of my accident, while I was meditating and feeling my feelings deeply, a vision came to mind of that thirty-three-year-old man lying on the table in an emergency room and lying in bed at Jefferson Hospital several days later. I remembered how scared and alone that young man was.

And then I experienced myself lying next to him in bed, holding him in my arms, kissing his head. Knowing that he would be okay and knowing that I couldn't tell him that. Knowing that he was going to have so much more pain and loss in life and knowing I couldn't tell him that either. Just holding him and loving him.

That's what I needed thirty-three years ago. That's what we all need. But there's a time when we stop demanding it of our spouse, our parents, or our god—and just know that it's in there. And when we know that it's in there, we can meet any other human being and look them in the eyes and know that we're looking at ourselves. Because the divine spark is in *there*—in that other human.

How can we *not* care?

VULNERABILITY

My friend Edward has worked his way up to become head of product development in a highly competitive multinational company in New Jersey. He's smart, very driven, and his rise in the corporate structure has been what they call "meteoric." Because I happen to know a number of people in the company, I know that he isn't particularly well liked, but I'm also aware that this is no secret to him.

During the few times we've talked about his business, Edward has described how embattled he feels when dealing with his line staff and even senior management. He has hundreds of people reporting to him and feels he must constantly push them to work harder or else the job will never get done. So you can imagine how a staff of professionals feels about that! No surprise, he pushes himself even harder than he does the staff and he doesn't let up. So the harder he pushes, the more he appears to be insensitive and not respectful. (One of the people I know at the company described him as a heartless son of a bitch.)

On the other hand, there is another side to Edward. He has told me about how much anxiety he feels whenever he has to speak to the public—which he does pretty often—and how insecure he is about many things in his life. He told me that part of the reason he drives himself is because he's afraid of losing his job, that he's been afraid of losing his job *throughout his whole career.*

Now, I happen to know that only someone with a beating heart feels that kind of anxiety. What he's talking about is fear of failure in front of others. And I know that people who are afraid of being shamed try to keep those emotions at bay. It's so frightening to face those emotions directly, so we turn our backs on them, strap on our armor, and push harder. I'm sure you know how effective that is. Unfortunately it works in the short run. But nobody has ever been smart enough, fast enough, or creative enough to outsmart their own mind!

At the risk of sounding arrogant, I think I know the cure. . . .

"You know," I said, "If your team knew this, they might like you better."

He laughed. "If my team knew this, they would cut me off at the knees!"

Recalling this conversation now, I wonder whether maybe Edward was right—in certain contexts, anyway. Among some species of animals, the ones that are most vulnerable become lunch for others. Bullies take advantage of the most vulnerable, as do pedophiles and psychopaths. But all of that is not typically how humans respond to visible vulnerability. Not in my experience, anyway. The vast majority of the time, it goes the other way; the ones who are vulnerable are embraced and cared for. I'm not really in a position to say whether the people reporting to Edward would take advantage of his vulnerability and cut him down to size or show greater consideration and concern for him if he revealed what was going on inside himself. But I do know, from what he said about being "cut off at the knees," that he is afraid to *show* his vulnerability. And that doesn't have to do with the responses of others. That has to do with a very human fear of exposure.

Whether or not other people can handle our vulnerability with understanding, most of us are not ready to do that for ourselves. As a matter fact, most of us find vulnerability intolerable. That fear probably originates in our primordial brains: we feel we are at risk of being destroyed if we are vulnerable. So when we are afraid of that, we work hard to appear strong or independent. We say things like, "I'm fine, thank you," or, "I don't need your help right now, but I'll keep you posted."

When I am in public among people who pretend not to see me, I know the reason is related to that fear. I am most people's nightmare. I am dependent and vulnerable. So if people are turning their backs on their own vulnerability, of course they turn their backs on me. What they are turning their backs on is what feels intolerable. Especially in today's culture.

But is it?

※　※

In the early days after my accident, whenever someone said they wanted to have lunch or dinner with me, I felt I needed to prepare them by reading down a list of everything I would need and everything that could happen. I would talk about how I would need help getting my coat off and on, that my food would need to be cut, my catheter bag might need to be emptied, that I might feel unwell (a.k.a., have an anxiety attack) and need to leave early. The implied question, at the end of my soliloquy, was, "After hearing how vulnerable and dependent I am, do you still want to go out with me? Do you still want to be my friend? Can you put up with my 'stuff'?" It may have seemed silly to run through the logistics like that. But behind it all was the question: "Given what I need, given all the things I can't do for myself, are you sure you want to be with me?"

Of course I needed their reassurance. After all, I found my dependency and vulnerability so shameful it was almost reprehensible. I couldn't tolerate my own neediness, so how could they? I felt like such a burden when I had to ask for help getting in and out of a restaurant or having my food cut or my jacket taken off and put on. It was so embarrassing to me, I wanted to scream. In those early years, I felt so full of shame, I felt like people were staring at me, and all I ever wanted to do was go home and hide.

I felt such intense hatred for my own vulnerability that I had aggressive, even violent urges. As we know from the news, shame and humiliation can produce angry and violent reactions. Of course there was no one to be angry with, so I just took my anger out on my broken dependent body. There were times when I was alone and I would pound my legs in anger. Of course I didn't feel any better, just sad. So very sad, impotent, and alone.

Then there was my therapy practice. Before my accident I read a great deal and even gave talks about the value of the vulnerable therapist. But it's so easy to talk about the virtues of being vulnerable when you are still under the illusion that you are *not* vulnerable. What happens when it's absolutely impossible for a therapist to hide his vulnerability?

This was uncharted territory. I was scared when I first returned to the office and began seeing patients. I recall the first therapy session after my accident, pushing my wheelchair down the hallway on my way to see that first couple. It felt like a life-or-death moment. I was insecure anyway, but what if I were rejected by my patients on top of it all? How would my patients receive me? I was supposed to be caring for them—but here I was, so broken. How could they trust me or feel safe with me?

From the age of twelve, all I wanted to do was be a psychotherapist. I had begun to be pretty good at it. And because that had been the focus of my attention, it was really all I knew how to do for a living.

Even after a number of sessions with patients, the feelings of exposed vulnerability and shame did not go away. One of my early patients coming into my office glanced at my wheelchair and asked, "What kind of chair is that?"

I got defensive, fearing that she was judging me.

"Why do you want to know?" I asked.

Very casually she replied that her sister was in a wheelchair and mine looked much more sophisticated.

I think you could have heard my sigh throughout the building! So my vulnerability was no big deal to her. My patient had come for therapy, and that's what she wanted. Little did she know that what just happened was incredibly therapeutic *for me*. Finally I could relax and we could just be humans in the room.

It was as if she were saying, "I know you are vulnerable and dependent, that's no big deal. I need your help, let's get started." With that came the realization that my relationship with my patients had begun to change. It was the beginning of a process that has represented some of the most valuable learning of my entire life.

❧   ❧

Slowly I grew into becoming more comfortable as a vulnerable therapist. Today I experience myself as both vulnerable and comfortable; my patients feel the same about themselves. We begin as kindred spirits—two vulnerable human beings sharing openhearted space, something I consider sacred space.

During a session, I frequently have to ask my patients to help me with my beverage, to open a window, or to excuse me when my blood pressure goes up and my catheter has to be checked. I can't even remember how many times I've dropped something on the floor or spilled my beverage on myself. Several times, my leg bag has leaked all over the floor while I was in session. It even happened twice with the same patient! (I thought about terminating her prematurely, thinking she might have bad catheter karma!)

What has happened is that many of my patients feel deeply caring toward me. When things happen to me, their response is about me and not them. They feel deeply when I suffer, and they want to help. They are protective of my health, so they cancel sessions when they have a cold—or what could become a cold—because they don't want me to catch the bug. When we start a session and they say to me, "How are you?" they mean it. It's not just the fact of my vulnerability that makes them feel safe, it's my comfort with my own vulnerability—my gratitude for the life I have—making them feel safe and hopeful. Just as important, my vulnerability has enabled them to feel a kind of compassion that is one of the building blocks for well-being.

※ ※

Dr. Brené Brown, a research professor at the University of Houston, has studied vulnerability for the last ten years. (The video of her "TED talk" on this subject has become immensely popular—viewed by well over six million people.) Brown suggests, and I agree, that you cannot have a truly intimate relationship without "vulnerability tolerance." And the more vulnerable we allow ourselves to be, the more intimate our relationships become. I have long said that the hunger to be known exceeds the hunger to be loved. If we don't feel known for who we are, in the deepest sense, love cannot penetrate. If someone says they love us but does not know our darkest side, our fears, our fragility, our areas of shame and hostility, all they can love is what we show. If we don't communicate to them that we are sometimes "full of shit," then we live in fear that we will be rejected if they see this side of us.

And for anyone in an intimate relationship, the learning never ends. However close and loving we are with someone else—physically and emotionally—there is always the question of how comfortable we are with ourselves.

※ ※

As I write, I am in a relationship that is unlike any other I have experienced since my wife left me twenty-four years ago. I first met Joan when she was assigned as a weekend nurse. When I saw her walking down the hall toward me—an attractive woman with a radiant smile —I immediately felt warm and relaxed. My response was unusual because typically when I see a new nurse I feel some anxiety, wondering if she will get things right and if our personalities will match. I didn't feel any of that with Joan, I just smiled reflexively. All that, without saying a word.

Well, Joan and I have a lot in common. We share similar values. Both of us have two daughters we love. Like me, Joan is a student of meditation and a baseball fan. Over the first year or so, we found that we loved to just hang out and talk. Slowly, we both realized we were falling in love.

Joan is attractive, spiritual, insightful, reflective, and about as neurotic (meaning anxious and insecure) as I am. When we talk about what attracts us to each other, she tells me about the qualities in me that she finds endearing or praiseworthy. And yet the question still looms. What about my perceived imbalance in our relationship—where she has to put my coat on, get my beverages, do most of the driving! I ask the looming question, Joan minimizes it, and I don't know how to pursue it. And even when I don't ask it, shadows of my past fears and insecurities still linger. She knows *my* vulnerability and insecurity and fear. And she knows, when I express my fear of being a burden, those shadows are back and I am feeling vulnerable and insecure. Sometimes when I am conscious of those feelings, I just tell her, "I think I am a quart low on serotonin today!"

And when Joan says to me, "Do you still love me?"—or when she tells me she couldn't sleep the night before because she was angry at someone and couldn't stand being angry, or when her eyes tell me that she is sad or frightened—I know she's a quart low also. And like all other humans, when we feel vulnerable, we really need to be held either physically or emotionally.

But there's another dimension to that need. Not only do we want compassion from others, we also want it from ourselves. Can you be vulnerable and feel compassion for yourself at the same time? Can you look in the mirror and say, "I don't know what to do. I don't have the answers. I need help. I'm vulnerable and insecure and human." Can you embrace that figure you see in the mirror and do it with the same compassion my patients feel toward me, the same compassion we all feel toward someone we care about who is feeling fragile, the same compassion that is the beginning of a life of kindness and joy?

PLEASE HELP ME

The couple had been married for twenty years. For both Geraldine and Richard, it was a second marriage, and retirement was just over the horizon. Both were under a great deal of stress. Richard's company was moving its headquarters, and if he was going to keep his job he and Geraldine would have to make the move. Neither one wanted to move, but they could not afford to retire right away.

This situation could not have come at a worse time. Geraldine's daughter had a troubled teenage son who had just been arrested on a drug charge. The daughter lived close by, and Geraldine wanted to do everything she could to help her daughter and grandson through this difficult time. Her grandson was out on bail and was facing a possible prison term. Her daughter was raising him alone and had limited social and economic resources. Geraldine felt that her daughter and grandson needed as much of her help as she could give, but she was meeting resistance from a daughter who was so vulnerable and ashamed, she wouldn't let anyone in. Geraldine felt closed out, and that only added helplessness to her fears.

So Geraldine's days were filled with worry as she could not take her mind off this situation. The more she thought about it and the more she envisioned catastrophic scenarios, the more frightened she became. And although she was able to function, she spent most of her mental energy ruminating by herself. So by the time Richard came through the door at the end of a long day, Geraldine was ready to explode; she immediately started giving him the latest updates, expressing her fears and nightmare scenarios. She couldn't see that when Richard arrived home he was tired and stressed. Geraldine was so frightened and needy, she felt that all she needed was a best friend who would listen to her. Because of her intense anxiety, all she could experience was her own distress, and all she wanted was some temporary relief. Like most humans she looked for relief by telling her story to another person. That was Richard.

But because she was so focused on herself, she was unable to see that Richard was suffering. If she had been calmer, she could have seen the stress in his eyes, the tension in his shoulders, and his overall exhaustion. But the focus of her attention, understandably, was on her own fears. She couldn't know that Richard was trying to maintain his performance objectives while making arrangements to move to the home office. All this would have been difficult and stressful enough for a much younger man; it was even more so for a man nearing seventy with diminished stamina. So when Richard came home, he was looking for respite. But instead he found his wife (who was also his best friend) beside herself with fear and anxiety, looking to him to carry her through this stressful time. He did his best to listen to her, as he himself wasn't even aware how tired he was when he got home.

When this couple came to see me, it didn't take long to get a picture of their usual evening ritual. When Richard came home "after a long, hard day at work," he would listen to Geraldine for a few minutes, then would go to the kitchen and pour himself a glass of Scotch before he went back and listened to Geraldine's worries some more. His intentions were good. He understood what Geraldine was going through. After all, he had been a stepfather to her daughter since she was an adolescent. He and Geraldine had always been involved in their grandson's life. So he too was worried.

Despite his exhaustion, Richard tried to be loving and understanding. Yet Geraldine felt that he listened without fully listening. Richard admitted that this was so. He was looking forward to pouring himself another Scotch.

Geraldine was grateful to Richard for *trying* to listen. But it wasn't enough. Without any real involvement or response from him, her anxiety remained undiminished. At the same time, Richard continued to feel alone in his own process of transition. But he couldn't feel that emotion because he was busy trying to be the good husband. And without really knowing it, he was using alcohol to help him.

As pressures mounted, Geraldine had begun overeating. And she knew why. Food calmed her; eating seemed to take a pressure off for a little while. But she was putting on weight, it was beginning to show, and that only made her feel more out of control.

During an early session, we revisited the moment when Richard would walk in the door and pour his first glass of Scotch. I reminded him of the words he used to describe that—"after a long, hard day at work."

"Before you walk in the kitchen," I asked, "what is it like to live inside of your skin at that moment? What does your *body* feel like at the end of a long, hard day? We know that your mind wants you to be a good husband, but what does your body want?"

He couldn't answer. (Sadly, that's the way most people respond. When we take a minute to reflect, we know we need something but we don't quite know what it really is.)

So I said to him, "What do you feel when you come in the house and you begin to hear her story, her distress?"

We stayed with the emotions. After a moment's reflection he was able to say that he felt great tension across his forehead. And then? While he rubbed his forehead, he described how that tension moved down his cheeks to his chest. When he did, he was visibly distressed.

I asked, "Then what does your body need?"

With his eyes closed, he responded, "I need my forehead touched."

What could they do?

Richard's body was saying, "Please help me, please hold me!"

And as Geraldine and I spoke about what she really needed, she realized that talking about her fears and anxiety with Richard didn't make her feel any better. If anything, it made her feel worse. The way she described it, it was almost like scratching skin that was inflamed with poison ivy. The more you scratch, the worse it gets, and the more difficult it is to stop scratching. And when she listened to Richard describing his internal experience when he came home, she realized that that was exactly what *she* needed when he came home—to be touched, to be held. She had believed that her words would "get through" to him, and once they did she would feel better. But now she knew she wanted what most of us want when we feel distress—we want to be held.

As Mark Nepo described in the poem "Accepting This":

My efforts now turn
from trying to outrun suffering
to accepting love wherever
I can find it.

❀　❀

Richard and Geraldine were sitting together on the couch in my office, close but not touching. I asked them to not say anything and just look into each other's eyes.

Richard moved his hand over to touch Geraldine's. Both of their shoulders seemed to drop a bit and he put his arms around her. But when he did, she looked at me and began to explain, "As soon as I feel held, I start thinking about my daughter and how she doesn't have this respite in her life."

I pointed out what had just happened—that as soon as she felt her body, she went right into her head. (That's not unusual, as our pattern of thinking is habitual. So Geraldine's brain was in the habit of focusing on what was wrong in her life. In this moment of respite, her mind did what it may have been doing for the last fifty years.)

I gently brought her back to what was happening in her life right at that minute: "Your body is calling to be held. Let yourself

---

*Mark Nepo, "Accepting This," www.marknepo.com/poems_accepting.php

feel Richard's touch. Let yourself rest on his shoulder. Feel your arms around his waist pulling him closer. Notice the experience of your whole body."

I asked them to do it again—to hold each other. And this time, to do it mindfully—to feel each other's hands on their shoulders or waist, to feel their partner's cheek, the temperature, the texture, to feel the rhythm of each other's breathing, and to allow their breathing to go in synch—even to feel each other's hearts.

"And when you move into your head," I said, "gently come back. Listen to the call of your body saying, 'Please return; please return.'"

Again they held each other, and it was for a long time. I saw the pain diminish in Richard's face. I saw Geraldine's breathing slow as she nestled her head in Richard's chest. Finally they had what they both wanted—connection.

And that connection could happen only after they heard the voices calling out from every cell in their bodies, voices they had learned to silence. Now those voices could be heard, saying softly but clearly, "Please help me."

❧ ❧

Brené Brown initially spent years researching how and why some people feel connected and others don't. Why do some people feel that they belong—while others feel that no one understands them? What is that unnamed thing, she asked, that nurtures or interferes with our connections to each other?

In time, she discovered her research leading her to an unexpected conclusion. What constantly got in the way of connectedness, she found, was shame—the repeated incantation in our brains, so common to us all, of "I'm not good enough, I'm not worthy enough, I'm not competent enough, I'm not smart enough. . . . "

So we live our lives feeling not quite worthy of what we most long for, and we devote our lives to fixing or hiding what we feel is broken. Shame causes us to hide—assuming that if anyone saw us for who we really were, we would be rejected.

Our instinct to hide our vulnerability may well be in our primordial genetics. A vulnerable animal in the wild would be rejected and left behind or become an easy lunch! But what I have discovered in my life and what Brené Brown discovered in her research was that the opposite was true.

In her book *Daring Greatly: How the Courage to Be Vulnerable Transforms the Way We Live, Love, Parent, and Lead*, Brown describes the moment when she met with her own therapist (Diana) and responded to the first question she posed.

"When do you feel the most vulnerable?" Diana asked her.

"When I'm in fear," Brown responded.** And then she went on to name every source of fear she could think of—feeling "anxious or unsure," having difficult conversations, trying things that are new, opening herself to criticism, revealing the depth of her love for her husband and children, trying to fix things that can't be fixed. And perhaps scariest of all, she concluded, "I feel it when I'm scared that things are too good."

After my accident, when my vulnerability was so visible, I didn't think I was unlovable, I *knew* I was unlovable, broken, and dependent. I knew I was worthless and less than human. All because my vulnerability was out there for the world to see; I no longer was able to hide.

**Brené Brown, *Daring Greatly: How the Courage to Be Vulnerable Transforms the Way We Live, Love, Parent, and Lead*, Gotham Books, 2012, p. 6.

Why do we try so hard to hide our own vulnerability? Why do a husband and wife have so much trouble saying, "I am hurting inside, please hold me"? Why is it so hard for so many of us to even allow ourselves to know that we want to be held? Why do we work so hard to hide our fears—not able to see that they are just part of being human?

For many of us, I suspect, the fear of vulnerability is a fear of rejection, or worse, humiliation. The children's story *The Emperor's New Clothes* is all about exposure and humiliation. We all laugh at the silly emperor who has no clothes. And yet if we truly know ourselves and each other, none of us has clothes—we are all vulnerable human beings. We are all ashamed of our dependency. We are all afraid of embarrassment or rejection. And I have yet to meet a human who doesn't have abandonment issues! And how about the universal fear of being inadequate, incompetent, or having no idea what to do?

But vulnerability is not weakness. Actually, acknowledging and owning our vulnerability takes great strength. How courageous it is when we look someone in the eye and say, "Please help me."

❧   ❧

Many summers ago, when my daughters were still young, my wife and I visited them at an overnight camp. It was a rainy day, and after we got back home and pulled into the garage, I realized the wheels on my wheelchair were still wet. While my wife and nurse went into the house, I stayed in the garage to dry the wheels, which I did by accelerating back and forth on the cement. At one point I switched from reverse to forward too quickly and I tipped over backward onto the concrete floor.

I was in agony. Lying on my back, alone, I thought I might have broken my collarbone. My house is fairly large and neither my wife nor my nurse was within earshot. So there I was, in terrible pain, assuming I was injured badly, and no one knew I was in trouble!

I didn't have to think about what I should do or say, or who would be listening, or what they might think when they found me like that. I just shouted—screamed—over and over again, with all the force in my weakened lungs, *"Please help me! Please help me!"*

There was a workman at my neighbor's house. He was the first to hear me and come to my rescue. He knelt down and put his hand under my bleeding head to see what I needed.

After that, it seemed only minutes before I was surrounded by people who wanted to help me.

Now, recalling that moment, I know how scared I was. I can relive the terror I felt while lying there, wondering who would hear me, who could save me. And I realize that every time I'm scared, these are the words that I either say aloud or that I want to say: *"Please help me!"*

I also know that this is not the cry of a victim. It is an affirmation. *Yes, I am vulnerable. I cannot do this myself. I need your help.*

This is where and how we connect. When someone looks at you and shows you their vulnerability, it opens your heart and both parties feel safer, more intimate. I watch it in my office all the time as couples share their deepest fears and longings with one another. Inevitably, this is followed by touch.

When we pretend we are stronger than we feel, we distance ourselves from each other. It's only through vulnerability that we can see another's tender heart. Although the research bears this out, I didn't need research to know it. I have been living it for over thirty years. I've watched people open their arms and their hearts as they face this vulnerable human. I don't know what I would do if I had the wherewithal to go on pretending I wasn't vulnerable. Thank goodness I don't have the option because now I am surrounded with love.

Our lives are intertwined, and that is what gives us strength. We need each other.

CREATE A MIRACLE

I usually get gas at the same neighborhood station. Lately, the same man has been pumping my gas, so we smile when we greet one another. He is a handsome young man with cocoa skin and a warm smile. Because my fingers don't work, he is always happy to help me get my wallet out and retrieve my credit card. Like many others, he is curious and amazed at how my van has been adapted so that I can drive while sitting in my wheelchair. And, also like many others, he seemed a bit uncomfortable about asking too many questions.

One spring evening when I was on my way home, I stopped for gas and we talked for about twenty minutes. I found out his name was Hari and he had emigrated from India several years before. His family still lived there. He was twenty-two years old and worked at the gas station fourteen hours a day. When he was done at work, he would ride his bicycle to his apartment twenty minutes away. There, he just had time to grab a meal, shower, and get some sleep before he rose the next morning to repeat the cycle.

Hari told me he was lonely but said he didn't have time to meet anyone because he worked so much. I was heartbroken that this kind, bright, and handsome young man struggled so, just to stay afloat. My paternal instinct told me that he was much too young to be so isolated. I felt sad and, because of that, I felt my heart open a bit.

And then he asked me if the woman I had been with the other day was my wife. I said no, that she was my nurse.

"You need a nurse all the time?"

I replied that I did and watched the great sadness in his face as his eyes became moist. Then he began asking about my disability, and when he heard that I had been in a wheelchair for nearly thirty-three years . . . more sadness. He kept asking me about my physical limitations and finally had to walk away for a few seconds because he was so upset.

When he came back, he leaned on my door.

I put my hand on his shoulder and said, "But Hari, I have something most people do not have. I am a happy man who loves many people. I wish that for you, my friend."

When we parted that evening, he called me his brother. Hearing that we were family, I dropped off a good deal of home-made food the next day. I told him that that's what it was like to have a Jewish brother!

So this is where we meet—with his life as an immigrant from India and my life as a quadriplegic. But just because we meet there, it doesn't mean we will stay there. Over the next few visits, I would hear a good deal more about his dreams and his fears. He would hear about what was exciting in my life and what was difficult.

And I was reminded of an oft-repeated phrase in the Hebrew Bible: "God Is One."

Many interpret this to mean that there is one God. And maybe that *is* what it means. (I'm certainly not a biblical scholar.) But perhaps it means that when people share a very intimate and human experience, we experience something sacred.

I have often referred to a Jewish parable that says that before an infant is born, an angel of conception infuses the infant with all of the wisdom he or she needs in life. And then the angel puts her finger on the child's lip and says, "Shhh," thus sealing a secret pact between that child and God. And as the story goes, that's why we all have that indentation on our upper lip. It's the angel's fingerprint!

May we all see the fingerprint on each other, whether we are Muslim or Christian or Jew, whether we are disabled or star athletes. I wish for all of us to have encounters like the one I had with Hari. May we all have more brothers and sisters and share a sacred experience.*

---

*Previously published in *The Huffington Post*, April 12, 2012

PART 5

Faith

THE LESSON OF THE IVY

The ivy plant was a cherished gift that came at a very difficult time in my life. Joan gave it to me on Valentine's Day, and it was in the shape of a heart. It was a sweet gift of life and love from a woman who means so much to me. I put it in my office on a windowsill near my desk so I could enjoy it every day.

To say this gift arrived at "a difficult time" is understating the case. For years I have had what you might call an evolving relationship with my body. Early on, after my accident, I hated it for all the ways it had broken down, failed me, refused to respond to what I felt were reasonable expectations, nearly lost some germ-warfare battles with treatment-resistant bacteria, and caused great suffering, not only for me but for my loved ones. I hated how, occasionally, my bladder or bowel would cause me terrible humiliation. As the years went on, I felt I was treating my body like a fickle lover who would sometimes respond and sometimes betray me.

But over the last ten or fifteen years, all this rage and resentment has gone away. Instead, I am filled with gratitude and awe—that my body has managed to survive its many misfortunes, engaged in repeated skirmishes with wildly aggressive bacterial and viral invaders, regenerated cells with tireless efficiency—and even, at times, provided moments of exquisite pleasure, ranging from the taste of excellent sushi to what I feel when embraced by another human being. When my body breaks down, I feel great compassion for the way it has worked so hard for so many years to give me the wonderful quality of life I have now—how it has enabled me to live beyond anybody's wildest expectations. I feel kindness toward this body that now suffers.

Not always, of course. It's not like my ego is gone forever. To be honest, there are still many times I get pretty pissed, especially when my body breaks down just when I'm about to carry out some wonderful plans. I can do self-pity as well as anyone! But eventually I reawaken to the fact that my body struggles and my ego is a brat.

※ ※

In the same month I received the ivy, unknown to me (but always dreaded by me), I was about to embark on a series of *very* bad days with this vulnerable body.

Around the Valentine's Day when I received the ivy, my nurse noticed a wound on my hip that was not healing. It is pretty common for people who sit in wheelchairs to get wounds on areas of their bodies that are weight-bearing. Because of pressure on the skin, sores develop. (Some heal on their own when the pressure is alleviated.) Mine was unusual in this respect. It showed up at the top of my femur right where the hip joint begins. This is an area that is not necessarily weight-bearing, so it was difficult to understand how the wound had opened up or why it was not healing.

After months going to multiple doctors and trying a variety of ointments and antibiotics without success, in early summer I went to a guy who specialized in people with spinal cord injuries. He felt around the area and said, "Of course it's not healing. You've got osteomyelitis. The bone is infected at the top of your femur."

After the tissue was cultured, I learned the infection came from the *E. coli* bacteria, which was already bad news. I get multiple bladder infections because my bladder is unable to empty completely. And after all these years, *E. coli* bacteria have permanently colonized my bladder, and we have an uneasy truce. (I liken the "truce" to the relationship between the man-eating Bengal tiger and the castaway Pi sharing a life raft in *Life of Pi*.)

What made this infection particularly bad news was that it meant *E. coli* was traveling throughout my body, and it signaled a warning that the bacteria could now infect me anywhere. It went without saying that the infection would have to be treated immediately, aggressively, with long-term intravenous antibiotics and a surgical procedure.

When my doctor gave me details of what that surgery would be and what would be required during the very long recovery process, I realized my body was going to need a lot of my cooperation to get through this. After the surgery, I would need to remain in bed for six weeks, lying on my back or right side (being turned every two hours). During that time, I would not be able to elevate my head more than thirty degrees. That was the worst part. It meant I couldn't read and I wouldn't digest food well. It meant daily bed baths and toileting. Anyone's digestive system works better when they can be upright and get the benefit of gravity. Lying prone, without the help of gravity, my whole GI system would be thrown off. Twenty-four hours a day, seven days a week, for six weeks.

When the doctor described to me what was coming up, I had an interesting reaction. I wasn't depressed or scared or angry, because I knew what was coming. So I didn't *fear* this happening. Something similar had happened to me about twenty years earlier, and I had anticipated being in this situation once again. (I knew it, because as we age our skin gets thinner, which puts us at more risk for breakdown.) As a result, I had already made arrangements to modify the size of my bedroom, making it a little bigger to accommodate a seating area for company. So in a way I felt ready, if not quite prepared. And I knew that my body would require a great deal of time and nurturing in order to help me return to the life I loved.

I'm lucky to have so much practice in meditation. Largely because of that, I felt I could approach this whole experience with a curious mind and an open heart. I wondered how I was going to react. I was fairly confident I would have periods of depression and despair, but what other experiences would I have? I had a feeling this experience would somehow change me, and I was curious about how. I wondered how long I would dwell in the neighborhood of resentment and self-pity, and I wondered the same about neighborhoods of gratitude and love. I wanted to observe all of that—trusting I would be spending time in many such emotional neighborhoods over the next six weeks.

And, I would have to make sure someone watered the ivy in my office during my absence.

The procedure was done, and I learned that the proliferation of *E. coli* in my body was extensive and the surgeon had to remove a good amount of tissue, including much of my hip bone. I also learned that I was quite vulnerable to subsequent infections. So after five unpleasant days in the hospital I was taken home by ambulance to begin healing. Sure enough, I watched what happened. For the first week or so, I focused mostly on my body—the digestive problems, the logistics of turning me, all that kind of stuff. My stomach was frequently upset, and I worried about whether my bowels would become unregulated. The whole experience was a learning curve, as I figured out how I could watch TV, set up audio books for myself, and eat my meals. I was exhausted. It's difficult to sleep when you are awakened and turned every two hours. And I noticed that, in a way, my exhaustion was helpful as my body and mind were almost too tired to be agitated.

Maybe a week or so went by like that, and then I found myself looking at the clock and starting to count the days and weeks. When I did, I felt impatient and agitated, wanting the time to pass more quickly than it did. I entered what Buddhists call "the Hell Realm." This happens to all of us when we want the moment we are in to be different from what it is (the very definition of impossibility).

I feel so fortunate that I didn't stay in that neighborhood—just visited every now and then.

Visitors came. My daughter introduced me to the Showtime series *Dexter*, and I got hooked—watching an entire season on DVD. A visit to the hospital, after three weeks, was a thrilling experience. When the ambulance arrived, I asked the EMT people to let me lie on the stretcher in the driveway for a little while so I could feel the sun on my face. And when the doctor said I was doing well, that now I could sit up to forty-five degrees for twenty minutes when I ate—well, now I know how the ancient Hebrews fleeing Egypt felt when the Red Sea parted. Talk about freedom!

And there were times when I shut down. There was one whole week when I felt myself getting small. What that means is, I didn't particularly want company. I didn't want to watch TV. I didn't want to socialize. It wasn't depression per se—that is, it didn't look or feel like it. I just felt myself getting small (I can't think of another way to put it), almost like my soul was going into hibernation.

After six weeks, I could begin getting out of bed—first, for twenty minutes twice a day, then three times a day, then for forty minutes three times a day—and so on.

The day I was allowed out of bed for forty minutes, I went into my office. It was the first time I'd been there all summer. I went in just to look around, but at once I noticed the ivy plant. It had developed a runner that wrapped itself around the handle of the blinds, wound its way up through the wooden slats, climbing all the way to the ceiling and then curling back down toward the window. It reinforced the awe I feel that life finds a way to continue living any way it can. Ultimately, we all need to grow toward the sunshine, just like my ivy.

And one more thing I noticed that we humans and this plant had in common: once this plant grew up beyond the wooden blinds and reached the ceiling, it stopped growing. It had nothing to cling to—nothing to hold on to.

I know the feeling. We all do. It is only with the support and the loving care of others that we can continue to grow and find our way to the light.

I looked at the ivy for quite a while, thankful for those who had watered it while I was recuperating. For the woman I loved, who had given me this Valentine's Day present. For the doctor who found the infection and knew what to do. For my nurses and visitors, and for the patients I would see again in this office where the ivy grew.

Before I knew it, my forty minutes were up. Time to return to my bed. My body needed some more care. And I had faith that, like the ivy, it would know what to do.

PARENTING: LIVING
BETWEEN FEAR AND FAITH

Parents worry, of course. That comes with the territory. Every parent I've ever met still remembers the first moment they saw their child—this beautiful, vulnerable human being who's now theirs. You greet this moment with breathless awe: it's an experience you've never had before and an experience you never forget. And a few seconds later, you feel anxiety.

As for what comes after that. . . . Psychologists and child-rearing specialists have provided lengthy lists of how-to's and shoulds and shouldn'ts. Libraries are filled with books about the intricacies of parenting infants, toddlers, and children of every age. And most parents today are keenly aware of the expert opinions, the news reports, and the warnings. How early education influences academic performance in later years. How a family environment affects relationships. You can compare a wide variety of philosophies regarding discipline and structure—how much is enough, how to maintain it, what is excessive. And when issues arise—physical, psychological, or generational—you can consult numerous sources for advice on what to do, how to handle situations, what works and what doesn't, where to go for further assistance.

Concerned parents today have resources like never before. Nearly all our anxieties about our child's present or future can be addressed in some form. Which is not to say the anxiety will ever be relieved. As we glean advice, expertise, and experience from many sources, it is all with the hope that our kids are okay and always will be. It's with the hope that we won't have to worry so much about them. And yet, inevitably, that's what we do.

And in today's twenty-four-hour news cycle, anxiety seems much worse. We hear about each incident of child abuse, abduction, freak injury, or illness so often that we come to believe all of these parental nightmares are just around the corner.

Our survival as a species has often depended on our fear, wariness, and our alertness to danger signals. Back when we were roaming the forests and savannahs, trying to evade savage bears and mountain lions, *Homo sapiens* had senses like alarm signals. Our ancestors had to remain alert to anticipate man-eating predators and heed dire warnings before it was too late. So when we hear these reports about all the dangers our children could be exposed to, it stirs up these primordial fears. We are cautioned about too much digital technology, too much sugar, too much peer pressure, too much parenting. Or we are cautioned about too little structure, too little exercise, too little supervision, too little discipline, or too little parenting. We are buffeted by messages from news media and mental health professionals, all telling us what we should be worried about. So we worry . . . and then we worry some more.

But what about that breathless *awe*? What happens to *that*? It doesn't go away, but it does get silenced by our anxiety. As soon as a child leaves the crib, do we turn all our attention to *what happens next* (the source of anxiety) rather than *who this child is* (the source of awe)? So much of our parenting originates from fear—which really comes from our own anxiety. But anxiety is simply a piece of information. Sometimes that information is valid; it helps us recall our child's doctor's appointment or prompts us to remember to call the teacher about an issue our child might be having. But the vast majority of the time, anxiety brings us no valuable information. It's just fear of a mountain lion you're probably never going to encounter—fear that's either created by the news or by our own fertile minds. And whenever we feel anxiety, we suffer.

What is the opposite of fear? Faith. I'm not talking about faith in a higher being. I'm talking about faith in the human spirit of that precious child—faith that, ultimately, that child will be okay with a bit of guidance and a healthy supply of love. And with faith we begin to understand that despite the fear instilled in the primitive part of our brain, there is no mountain lion lurking around the corner. We begin to see future risks for what they are—not so much falling-off-a-cliff but more falling-down-and-scraping-a-knee.

Faith cures fear. Fear silences faith. Too often we raise our children based on fear. Being a parent of a vulnerable and spiritual being means being on the middle road between fear and faith.

Many of us start with an agenda: (1) to steer our children on the right path; (2) to keep them out of harm's way; (3) to make sure they learn what they are supposed to learn, get the education they are supposed to have, develop self-esteem, and live up to their potential. But what if our agenda could start with something else? What if our agenda was *being curious*? Asking ourselves . . . *Who is this child? How does he explore the world? What are her thoughts and feelings? How does his imagination work? What are her dreams? How will he unfold and blossom?*

Then our children can become our teachers. As my grandson Sam, and now Jacob, have become mine.

Whenever I've taken a cruise (which I've done several times), I've been pleasantly surprised by the wheelchair-friendly environment. Generally there's good access to staterooms, dining rooms, and balconies on board. There are plenty of people to help out with opening doors and managing logistics. Of course, some off-ship excursions aren't wheelchair friendly, and some ports of call have limited access, but on a well-equipped cruise ship I have almost as much freedom of mobility as in my own home.

When Jacob was about four years old, he and I went on a Disney cruise with his mother and my nurse. Jacob and I had a great opportunity to spend a lot of time together, and we made the most of it. He loved to sit in my lap while we were riding from place to place around the ship. Without prompting or instruction, he developed a very good eye for potential hazards. He loved to jump off my lap and show me where there was a lip in the doorway that I had to be careful about.

There was one particular ramp leading to a balcony that was pretty steep and difficult to maneuver, but Jacob knew just what I needed and would leap into action whenever we came to that ramp. He would jump off my lap, open the door, and remind me to go very slowly. When it was time to get snacks or drinks, he was literally my right-hand man. I would order the food and sign for it and then he would bring it to the table and unwrap the food for us. And with things he couldn't quite figure out, I was *his* right-hand man. We met the challenges and solved all problems together— and we both loved it.

But who taught Jacob to do all that? Certainly not I. All he and I were doing was hanging out together. No one ever gave Jacob instructions on being loving or compassionate. No one told him to look out for me or scan the path ahead for trouble spots. Jacob didn't need obedience lessons, nor was this the kind of stuff that he could sit down and memorize. For our life together on the Disney ship, there was neither script nor scripture. Whatever Jacob had to figure out, he figured out by himself. He was just Jacob being Jacob.

Jacob is not unique in this way. When my grandson Sam was younger, he devoted a great deal of time and energy trying to figure out how I could hang out on the beach with him. When my niece Chelsea was about seven years old and we went out to dinner, she would stand next to me to open my straw and put my napkin on my lap, and she wouldn't sit down until she knew I was comfortable. Though all three of these children are family, I don't think that makes them more remarkable than other young people. There is something inside of all children that guides them toward care and kindness.

❦   ❦

Those rich memories came back to me when I attended an eight-week seminar on teaching meditation. Although there was a book assigned and an overall structure, there were no lists of things to memorize and remember. It was mostly experiential. To the consternation of some attendees, it became clear that the instructor was not going to let us take notes. Quite a number of people in the class expressed frustration. They had come to this class with notebooks in hand and goals in mind and did not want to leave empty-handed. As a matter fact, some said they were expecting a package describing what to do when teaching a mindfulness meditation class.

With quiet firmness the instructor engaged in a discussion about what this class required. "You won't need notes," he said. "All you need to do is be present. You have to be centered and awake." And as the discussion continued, he made the comment, "You can't teach this stuff from your head. It just won't work. It has to be taught from a position of mindfulness."

As I listened, it occurred to me how difficult this kind of assignment would be for anyone who came with the expectation of learning lessons, mastering techniques, engaging in a practicum, and passing with flying colors. Of course there would be things we needed to learn, and they would be handed to us later. But the actual teaching had to come from our hearts and not our heads.

Some of my fellow students, however, were used to the things most students are used to: "Here is the material. Study it, learn it, and repeat it back at the end, and you will either get a passing grade or a failing grade." That wasn't the situation here. None of us was going to pass or fail. There would be no exam. Voices would be heard, feelings would be aired, conflicts might or might not be resolved. None of us would leave the classroom with mastery of love, kindness, and compassion. None would make the grade to become skilled meditators. All we would have was this experience of each other and ourselves.

So much of parenting, so much of life, is like that meditation class. When there is conflict, we don't always need to fix it. First we need to be able to tolerate the distress associated with conflict. We need to be awake to our own experience rather than living in our heads, automatically trying to make repairs. When we fully experience our lives, we will be able to tolerate conflict more and be able to *do less* and *experience more*. You see, *not* fixing things requires a great deal of faith—that voices will be heard, feelings will be aired, and the mountain lion will not appear. Faith is really about releasing our grasp on what we have been doing automatically for so many years.

Our job as parents is to hold the child who's in pain, who's angry, who's confused, who rails against injustice, who has been reprimanded by a teacher, bullied, failed a test. To hold that child who needs our help, our care, our compassion—and who also needs our faith. Children need our understanding that, no matter what happens, they are simply *doing life*. They need to know there's wise, loving companionship in their parents—that there's a bottom they'll never fall through. They need our guidance, but if we act out of our own anxiety, we will raise theirs. If we can hold their pain, we can teach them to tolerate their own painful emotions. And then we can make decisions together about what is best in a particular situation.

We cannot do that without faith. And we cannot have faith in our children unless we have faith in ourselves. That means understanding what we have inside—knowing the wisdom we're born with. It means knowing that we have the same spirit inside that Jacob, Sam, and Chelsea have. It means being able to look into our own eyes and see something that's been in there since the first moment we saw those eyes—something that will be there forever, for us, with us, and with our children.

THE QUIET TRUTH

I have a dear friend, Noreen, whose son Josh is severely autistic. When her husband died six years ago, her son was only eleven and Noreen thought she could still manage him. Now that the boy is seventeen and much bigger and more aggressive, it has become clear to Noreen she can no longer keep him at home and also protect her two younger children.

As painful as placement is, the economics and the politics can be just as difficult. By law, school districts have to pay for residential treatment if they can't educate a child in a classroom setting. In today's economy, with public schools under great financial stress, schools do everything they can to avoid the extra financial burden of placement.

So now, in addition to the heartbreak of finding a place for Josh outside her own home, my dear friend has to convince the school district that her son is so out of control that he cannot be educated in the school setting. The fact that he could be a threat to her and her other children does not come into play in this discussion, so she has to convince the school district that he could be threatening to his fellow students and teachers. (By the way, this is the dilemma most parents face when they have a child who is "classified.") In addition, now she has to convince Medicaid that it is unsafe to keep him in the home and that he requires professional residential care appropriate for someone with autism. And in order to do that, the parent has to focus attention on her own child's weaknesses rather than his strengths.

So here she is—a kind, well-organized, extremely competent woman who has to face two public agencies, both of which are dedicated to the welfare of children, and convince them that her son can no longer live in the same house with her. Out of concern for his welfare and the safety of herself and her other children, he needs to be placed in another residence. As Noreen began to explore the steps to be taken, it turned out that the Medicaid case manager was completely on board. But nothing could be done until the school district agreed to pay for the educational component.

Noreen requested a meeting with the head of special education for the school district, a woman she had known and worked with very compatibly for many years. Noreen wanted to engage this other woman as her partner. And even though Noreen had retained a lawyer upon my recommendation (well, okay, my *insistence*), she chose to go into this meeting alone.

When Noreen arrived, there were several people in the room, two of whom she had never seen before. Despite that, she made her case with an open heart, a sense of gratitude, and a wish to engage.

After the meeting, she called me and we talked about it. She told me she felt they listened carefully yet gave her all the reasons why they *shouldn't* and *wouldn't* pay for the placement of Josh in a residential setting. When we spoke on the phone, she was crying. All I wanted to do was hold her. She had been alone with this stress for so many years, and now she had to place her firstborn son outside of the home. She carried all of the guilt any mother would, and then she convinced herself that her late husband would be heartbroken if he knew what was going on. I could almost feel through the telephone how overwhelmed this kind and loving mother was.

Though I rarely offer advice, I know there are times in our lives when we all need to be carried, and this was such a moment for Noreen. I told her that she should never—and *would* never—be alone in those meetings ever again.

She cried and said, "It's not my style to be adversarial and threatening."

Of course she didn't even have to tell me that. I knew that wasn't her style. She imagined herself in a setting where she could get what she wanted for Josh by engaging and listening to people who would share her feelings about this difficult situation. Perhaps they would not fully understand how difficult this was for her, but at least they would respect the depth of what a mother must be feeling and acknowledge that she could no longer care for the son she loved so completely. And now, her experience with the school officials was telling her that such a path was impossible. Still reeling from the meeting, her racing thoughts and intense emotions had her in turmoil. If she was going to get what she needed, she knew she would have to do something differently. She would not get what she wanted without forcing the issue.

In a phone conversation it wasn't possible to look into her eyes. But even without that direct connection, I could feel myself holding her gently. I knew she was feeling weak and was turning to me as I had some experience and resources to offer her. Not only that, she was beginning to understand how much I cared for and about her. So after we discussed some of the details of what needed to be done, I invited her to just listen to my quiet voice and *feel herself* being held and cared for. I could hear by the diminished speed and intensity of her speech that she was beginning to let go and rest. I asked her to just notice her breath every time she exhaled and just let go a little more. At that moment there was nothing to do and nowhere to go; she just had to experience being with me in the context of our conversation. And toward the end of our conversation when everything was quieter, I suggested that beyond her racing thoughts and intense emotions, perhaps underneath it all, she *knew* what would happen. She knew that Josh would be placed in residential treatment. To know this, she did not have to remake herself into an expert combatant with legal expertise to vanquish the decision makers. Next time she met with school officials, she would need to have her attorney along to do whatever fighting needed to be done. And she would undoubtedly need the support of others in her family.

Noreen could not possibly anticipate what would happen in the weeks and months that would follow, what the "fight" would look like, or what would happen during forthcoming meetings and discussions. She had little control over the challenges that lay ahead. What she did have was her silent truth. She could approach every meeting *knowing* what was going to happen. You see, when she settled into her experience, she knew her son would be *placed*, and she also knew that placement was the right thing for everyone. She didn't know what the process would look like, but in her heart she knew what the outcome would look like. That was her quiet truth.

❧ ❧

What would that be like for her? What does it mean to approach an encounter knowing your own quiet truth? I told her a story from my own experience.

The year before, I had a large water leak in my house causing lots of damage, and because there had been stagnant moisture, I had mold in the walls and ceilings. What would it take to clear out the mold and make repairs? I got an appraisal, as did the insurance company, and work commenced. Only after the project had begun did we discover some further intransigent problems. The damage was more widespread than first estimated. Clearing out the mold would involve substantial additional expense. The insurance company balked, citing their original estimate. They refused to consider additional reimbursement.

That's when I called the claims adjuster. I asked to speak to the head of the department. After I introduced myself, I asked if he was familiar with the damage. He was. I told him how happy I'd been, over the years, with his company.

And in a calm, measured voice I told him he had a decision to make. This work was going to get done. My home would be restored. That was my quiet truth. I didn't have to convince anybody, because I knew the outcome and so did he. And now he had a choice about *how* it would get done. Would we work together or be adversaries?

I said, "I am really good at partnerships and working with you. I can be open and flexible and understanding." Then I added, "I am also a very good adversary." And I quietly explained that I could be aggressive if need be. I described to him what it would be like if I ended up in court with an attorney discussing mold remediation. I concluded by saying, "I appreciate your time, and I look forward to getting this project done."

I did not hear from him again. The job got done. Most of the expenses were paid by the insurance company, with the exception of a few repairs that they said were not associated with the damage and therefore not reimbursable. I thought those decisions were reasonable and didn't argue with them.

In telling this story to Noreen, I omitted a great deal—the many times when I felt discouraged or was angered by the pace of the repairs, as well as the logistical challenges of my domestic and professional life in the midst of all this disruption. Ultimately, none of that turmoil would affect the outcome. Because I knew my quiet truth. The work would be done. The repairs would be made. I was not going to spend the rest of my life in a house with mold.

❀ ❀

Noreen knows she is not going to spend the rest of her life with a young man who is out of control and occasionally violent. I know she knows—but only when everything gets quiet.

Beyond the racing mind, beyond the intense emotions, *we know*. Beyond what we fear or fantasize or wish for—inside, where it's quiet, *we know*.

That knowledge, that wisdom, is what I compared earlier to a boulder in the ocean. The boulder is unmoving when the waters above are rough, stormy, threatening, even dangerous. There is something deep inside each one of us that's quiet, that's solid, that *knows*.

By the way, Josh was placed at a residential facility and Noreen tells me he has never looked healthier or happier. She is relieved and grateful. She knew her quiet truth, and so did I. We all do . . . when everything gets quiet.

GENESIS REVISITED

People approach Bible stories in a variety of ways. Some try to find lessons. Others search for definite statements of God's will. Still others seem to relish discussing them: I've been in situations where the "meaning" of each episode of the Bible was argued back and forth among scholars and clergy who seemed to take great delight in the passion of the debate.

However we approach these stories, there is often an added complication. It's the problem of traditions. Yours, mine, the ancient world's, the modern world's, the secular, the sacred, and the profane. Those who have heard these stories before have heard them in some previous context, and that context may determine for the rest of our lives how we interpret them.

A biblical scholar, author, and psychotherapist, Naomi H. Rosenblatt, makes a strong case for Bible stories having a permanent place in our lives. In her book *Wrestling with Angels*, coauthored with Joshua Horwitz, she writes: "One of the unexpected surprises one discovers in the Bible is that men and women have been challenging God's authority ever since their creation. Absolute trust in God is the rarest form of faith. Wherever you may find yourself on the spectrum of belief in or about God, some character in the Bible has been there."*

I am not a biblical scholar, but from what I know of the stories, I find them to be wonderful allegories about birth, life, relationships, and death. God, certainly, plays a leading role. Faith, and what it means, is an ongoing concern. I know these issues are part of what has made the Bible the leading best seller in the Western world. But the other element, as Rosenblatt points out, is relevance. Wherever we are in our lives, "some character in the Bible has been there." These stories are universal. In biblical figures, we see ourselves. In their troubled and sometimes contentious relationships with God (or any other form of greater wisdom) and each other, we find the reflection of what it's like to struggle and contend with forces beyond our control.

And, please note, nothing in the Bible or in the lives described there can be taken as a step-by-step guide to happiness or well-being. Stories with happy endings may satisfy Hollywood producers, but they do not endure to become bedside reading for generation after generation. Bible stories involve searching and longing. They tell of gaining faith and losing it. Of strength and weakness, of loyalty and betrayal, of human triumphs and failings, of great darkness with

---

*Naomi H. Rosenblatt and Joshua Horwitz, *Wrestling with Angels: What Genesis Teaches Us about Our Spiritual Identity, Sexuality, and Personal Relationships* (New York: A Delta Book, 1995), Kindle edition, location 186.

occasional rays of light, and of voices from above or within. The conflicts make them universal, rather than the resolutions. Thousands of years ago, our ancestors found themselves facing dilemmas that are with us today. Circumstances have changed; the human heart has not. We can still recognize our true selves.

❦ ❦

Consider how the story begins in Genesis with Adam and Eve and the Tree of Knowledge of Good and Evil. From the moment God creates this couple, they're negotiating their relationship, working out who makes decisions and how. And while Adam and Eve are in the process of doing this, God puts the Tree of Knowledge of Good and Evil right in the middle of the Garden. Right *there*, where they can't ignore it. He tells them what it is—a tree that gives them the wisdom to discriminate between good and evil. And he says, "Don't eat the fruit or I'll throw you out of the garden."

Here's my take on that. Far from being Original Sin, one has to wonder why God put the tree in the middle if He really didn't want them to eat the fruit. I assume the garden was pretty big; He could have put that tree somewhere else. And He created these beings and knew they had curiosity, so He knew what was going to happen. Of course, He *wanted* his children to be able to have the wisdom to discriminate between good and evil.

As Adam and Eve are negotiating their relationship, Adam's impulse is to do what he's supposed to do. Eve looks at the big picture, which is about what they need in life. So they eat the apple. And God puts them out. The way I see it, this was all a setup by a benevolent father who (1) wanted his children to have this wisdom; (2) wanted them to make up their own minds about whether to eat the apple; and (3) knew that they had everything they could need or want in this garden. And, because of (3), they were at risk of never leaving and never having their own lives.

So God created Adam and Eve, and after they had this wisdom, they were ready to leave the garden—a.k.a. the womb. Birth happens, the baby takes her first steps, and the journey begins.

Now fast forward to the story of Abraham and Sarah. Talk about negotiating relationships! Sarah feels guilty about being barren, so she tells her husband Abraham, as an act of selfless love, that it's okay for him to sleep with their Egyptian handmaid Haggar and have a baby with her. Abraham, like Adam, is compliant, so he does what Sarah invites him to do. And the result is that Abraham and Haggar have a son, Ishmael. Except this doesn't work out so well because, later on, Sarah finally gets pregnant by Abraham and gives birth to Isaac. Now that she is nurturing their own son, she feels great discomfort, even shame, at the sight of Haggar and Ishmael in her house. My guess is that, blinded by her own discomfort, she fails to see the humanity of this child of Haggar. Nor does she see the powerful personal relationship between her husband and Ishmael. She can only feel her own distress. So Sarah tells Abraham to banish Haggar and Ishmael. (How many of us, in the heat of an argument or when we are lost in a story of betrayal inside of our heads, fail to see the humanity of the other person and just react to our own distress?)

Abraham meekly protests, but he hears God's voice reassuring him that Haggar will be okay. (Actually I'm not sure whether he really heard God's voice or whether this was just Abraham reassuring himself.) And then Abraham is given a strange test by God—who orders Abraham to sacrifice his son Isaac. Ever compliant to God's wishes, just like he was with Sarah (both on the occasion of having a child with Haggar and on the occasion of banishing Haggar and Ishmael from their home), Abraham is about to carry out this deed when, at the last moment, God stays his hand and Isaac is freed. All this is the beginning of a deep division in Abraham's family. God says Ishmael will lead one great (Arab) nation and Isaac will lead another (Jew). And we know how that worked out!

This is what I love about these Bible stories. The conflicts, the issues, the family dynamics are just as present today as they were several thousand years ago. Abraham and Sarah are negotiating their relationship. Abraham appears to be compliant with Sarah's wishes—but is he? We don't hear about outward conflict between Abraham and Sarah. But I wonder what went on behind closed doors (more accurately, behind closed tent flaps). And we also have to look at the step-sibling conflicts, between the favored one (Isaac) and the one who has been banished (Ishmael).

I have fantasies of transporting myself back some five thousand years and having a family therapy session with these fine people. I wonder what it would have looked like and what we could learn from it.

Let's see.

❧ ❧

Our family therapy session starts with silence. I listen for the one who talks first because, often, the one who speaks first is the one in the most pain. Abraham speaks first. Not only is he in great pain, but he is also the patriarch. Abraham has a long history of compliance, and everyone else has come to this session because Abraham told them to.

When Abraham begins speaking, he opens up about the great guilt he has lived with for so many years. He feels guilty about so many things. About being unfaithful to Sarah, even though he had her permission to sleep with Haggar. About sending his precious son Ishmael away from his home. And he feels guilt for being so ready to sacrifice Isaac. He talks about the anguish and confusion he has felt for many years of his life. It's almost as though he wanted to go back to that tree in the garden to know the difference between good and evil, between right and wrong.

Abraham has done what God asked him to do, yet there's so much suffering in the wake of his decisions. He feels humbled, confused, and filled with remorse. And he cries. Abraham has the courage to be vulnerable in front of his family. Because of that, he becomes a role model for a different kind of strength and courage. He demonstrates to his family that you can be vulnerable and strong at the same time.

After a few minutes, through his tears, he apologizes to Ishmael, to Haggar, to Isaac, and to Sarah. As the room falls silent, almost everyone is crying as many of those people are hearing something they have needed to hear for many, many years. With the door open for people to share their stories—with Abraham as the role model for open vulnerability—Ishmael begins to talk about how much he loved Abraham and how he felt loved by his father. He talks about how safe and wonderful his early years were and how hurt and how frightened he was when his father banished him—how unloved he felt.

Ishmael goes on to say that his greatest pain is around his mother's suffering. He says to Abraham, "What you did hurt my mother. Nobody can bear seeing their mother hurt. I forgive you for what you've done to me. I can't forgive you for what you've done to my mother."

I compliment him for having the courage to stand up to his father—to defend his mother—and for having the strength to forgive his father.

Haggar speaks: "I've always been fond of you, Abraham. I

gladly welcomed you into my bed. I delighted in our closeness. And then I felt shame after I brought you Ishmael. I felt as though I was seen as nothing more than a whore. I wondered if I was really worthy of a place at your table—of a place in your life. When you sent us away, I was scared and deeply hurt, but . . . (and she turns to Ishmael) I want you to hear this . . . (she turns back to Abraham) I knew you and knew how tormented you were—how you were trying to do the right thing for your wife and for God. I could see in your eyes how much you suffered. I forgave you then, and I forgive you now. I know you are just a humble man trying to do the right thing like the rest of us."

As Abraham weeps, he thanks her for her understanding and forgiveness.

Haggar becomes the teacher in the family.

Isaac says he never really understood why he was offered up for sacrifice. He never understood why Haggar was sent away. And despite this, he always felt guilty—assuming that his stepbrother was suffering in the desert while he had the comforts that a young man needed. Whatever Isaac had, he says, he felt he should be sharing with Ishmael.

Sarah is the last one to speak. She turns to Haggar and says, "I have no right to ask you this. But please forgive me. Like Abraham, I tried to do the right thing by allowing him to have a son even though I was barren. I thought I was being selfless and generous. I thought I could love him and you. And yet when you and Ishmael came into my life, I felt such shame about what I couldn't produce and what you could. Your presence made me feel so inadequate— almost worthless. And when I had Isaac, all I really wanted to do was care for him and not deal with all of those shameful emotions. So instead of facing my pain, I had Abraham get rid of the people I thought were causing it. I only respected my pain and ignored yours. From the bottom of my heart, I am so deeply sorry for the pain I have caused you and Ishmael."

❧ ❧

A "successful" session?

I don't know. Certainly, afterward, they can go their own ways with less baggage. Perhaps each has a greater sense of well-being. There is more room in their lungs for air and more room in their hearts for love. The dictionary defines forgiveness as letting go of resentment—and to an extent, all of them have let go of some of their resentment. But the hardest type of forgiveness is the kind that Abraham has to deal with—and that's forgiving himself.

The whole story of Abraham and Sarah is heartbreaking. Here are two very good people who have tried to do the right thing. But they are still struggling—they always will. Like all of us, they have been cast out of the garden of earthly delights. For them and us there are no three or ten or twelve steps to happiness. They have lived with the knowledge of good and evil inside them, and that knowledge will be with them forever.

And with us all.

PART 6

The Divine
Spark

THE DIVINE SPARK IN
ALL OF US

In kabbalistic teachings, there's a wonderful story about an event that occurred at the beginning of humankind. In the process of Creation, emanations from God were formed into vessels. Then the Divine Light was radiated into the vessels, and they shattered. But something remarkable happened to each one of the shards from those shattered vessels. Each one became a soul that was implanted in each one of us.

According to this story, a spark of divine wisdom was placed inside each of us before we were even born. But at the moment of birth we enter a world that is confusing and chaotic. The spark inside of us is forgotten or hidden. But it's still there. And our task in life is to remember what we once knew—the divine wisdom that is within each one of us.

The Buddhists believe that everyone has a Buddha nature. That's similar to another kabbalistic teaching I've mentioned, which tells us that before a child is born God infuses that child with all of the wisdom they need in life. But when I first heard about that teaching, I didn't know in one version it had a second part. In that version, as a final send-off, it is said that before the child is born an angel comes down and slaps the child so they forget everything. (I have to wonder if that angel has some anger issues.)

On the surface, that doesn't make sense. Why would we get all that wisdom only to lose it at the last moment? Well, we really don't lose it, we just forget it. So perhaps the path to wholeness and well-being is about rediscovering what's already in there.

In my therapy and in my teaching, I believe I have never said one word to anyone that they didn't already know. But how *do* they know? Perhaps what I help do is open people's hearts wide enough so that they can look inside to reclaim what has been in there all along.

❦ ❦

I was thinking about this story the first time I met Paula, who came to see me for therapy. And as I saw more of her, and heard *her* story in the sessions that followed, I began to feel almost on a visceral level what it might be like to be Paula. When that happens, I feel even more curious and compassionate—and that moment was the first time in her life that Paula felt safe, understood, and cared for. So, the journey took on a different dimension. When we feel understood, really understood and safe at the same time, things begin to change. Shame and fear of judgment diminish, and the heart slowly begins to open. And we can only find our wisdom, compassion, love, and that divine spark when the heart is open. I knew we had embarked on an expedition together to reclaim some of that divine wisdom.

Paula was in her mid-forties. She had grown up in a home with a father who was sweet, but quite anxious. Paula described him as someone who allowed himself to be dominated by his wife, Paula's angry, depressed, hypochondriacal mother, Kristen. What was Kristen like? Paula portrayed her as extremely bright and intellectual. Her mother would not rage. Instead, she expressed herself in other ways that Paula remembered—talking about the darkness of life and imminence of her own death. Kristen was an avid reader, a scholar of sorts, and when she would tell Paula and her brother about the futility of life and how people were not trustworthy, she would comment about all of the brilliant writers and poets who thought the way she did.

Paula told me that when she was a child, she enjoyed life and liked people, but her mother convinced her that she was being naïve, silly, and childish. Her mother's dark brooding temperament couldn't tolerate any upset in the home; when Paula and her younger brother were laughing loudly, their mother would say they gave her a migraine and then would take to her bed, sometimes for several weeks, and refuse to talk to her children. So as a girl, Paula lived in fear of being bad and upsetting everything. And, as is typical of many firstborn daughters, she felt guilty and responsible for her mother's suffering.

Despite all her efforts to be good, during her childhood Paula was constantly criticized. This meant to Paula that she was failing in her efforts to protect her mother from suffering. That generated very harsh self-criticism. Now, as an adult, she lived with a great deal of anxiety and insecurity. She didn't trust her decisions and assumed that she was incompetent in many areas of her life.

Paula married a man who appeared pretty strong emotionally,

so the relationship initially helped this insecure woman feel more secure. After all, he took charge of everything. He paid the bills and managed the house. Stephen, her husband, was very controlling. He criticized the way she cooked, did laundry, even the way she washed the dishes. So Paula continued to feel small and incompetent. In a strange way this felt familiar and therefore okay. But after several years, she realized she was unhappy and that if she changed, she would be better and everything would be okay. She never gave up hope that one day she would finally get things right and not be criticized anymore. So when she was criticized by a mother or spouse or almost anyone, she assumed they were right. The self-criticism raged.

When she came to see me, she found her anxiety and critical self-judgment had become unbearable. She finally began to consider the possibility that her unhappiness was partly about her and partly about the way she had been treated. But she was too frightened to do anything about those feelings. Stephen was not really a tyrant, he was actually a nice person who was respected by his many friends. He taught business courses for high school seniors, and those students and teachers loved him. But when he was home, everything had to be just so, and he had little patience when it was not. Paula was a talented graphic artist, but her creative work did not free her. She said she always felt her work was not nearly as good as it should be. Of course she also felt that she wasn't as good as she should be, so of course anything she produced would not be good enough. And like anyone who is self-critical, she minimized whatever positive feedback she was getting and instead focused on what was wrong with what she was doing.

So there she was, in a marriage that was emotionally identical to her childhood. She and her husband had tried marital therapy several times over the years, with no change. In the first several months of our therapy, she said several times, "I know he will never change." But despite her words, she still had hope. And then one day she came to own that statement as her truth. That's when things got more complicated for her. She had little hope for her marriage, but because of her insecurity, she was too frightened to leave. Because of her history, she didn't trust that she was competent to live on her own. And the other reason was that she judged herself so harshly, she had no sense of whether her thoughts and feelings could be trusted.

I know that mind very well. I experienced that kind of insecurity, fear, and critical self-judgment when I was depressed. I was afraid to do almost anything because I knew I would screw it up. When people paid me compliments, I assumed they were lying just to make me feel better. But the difference between Paula and me was that I had a loving childhood, so I had better building blocks than she did. Trying to imagine living with that racing mind since childhood only made me feel more compassionate toward Paula. Sometimes when she spoke about what her mind was like, I was moved to tears as I had visions of a small girl feeling so scared and alone. And finally, when she saw that I was hurting, she realized how much she had been suffering and for how long.

Although trying to quiet a racing mind can be a fool's errand, I am of the firm belief that our minds are more cunning than we are! The work would begin with introducing Paula to her racing mind and simply observing all of the activity going on there. Anyone who engages in the activity of bearing witness to their own mind is astonished at how much is going on in there all the time. And over time, we begin to realize that most of what goes on there is pretty worthless.

I gave Paula an analogy I used in some of my earlier writings, when I compared the mind to a poorly functioning kidney. "You know, the kidney filters out the fluids that your body needs, and the rest of it is, well . . . piss. And most of it winds up in the bladder. The mind, on the other hand, is not so efficient. We have all of these thoughts, and we believe each one of them is important, so we chase them around inside our heads. But what we don't know is that ninety-five percent of these thoughts are really cognitive piss!"

It was so nice to see her laugh so deeply and heartily about the nature of her mind. That was the beginning of a phenomenon that could be lifesaving: perspective.

For Paula this realization initiated the process of helping her grow comfortable inside her skin. I was confident that once she was able to observe her mind without being a slave to it or taking it too seriously, critical self-judgment would diminish.

For most of us, it's too difficult to begin the process by observing our own mind. When we begin watching it, we inevitably get drawn back into it. So I taught her to pay attention to her whole experience, moment by moment. I began with inviting her to experience her whole body. First I had her close her eyes and become aware of what she was hearing in the room—my voice, the ambient sounds, birds singing—and then listen to the silence. I told her to pay attention with an "inquisitive ear" that listened for sounds; and then I told her to listen with a "passive ear" and allow sounds to come to her.

Next she learned to notice even more details about what she felt through her tactile senses—her feet on the floor, her thighs and buttocks resting on the sofa, the interlaced fingers of her hands. While her eyes were still closed . . . I asked how it felt inside of her mouth at the moment and the sensations on her tongue. What did she smell? Finally, I had her open her eyes just slightly as though she were seeing things for the first time. I wanted her to be aware of vision. I asked her to notice the colors, to focus on one item in the room and see as much detail as she could. And then, while she was looking at one item, I asked her to simultaneously be aware of everything her peripheral vision could see at the same time.

After we did that for a few weeks, with Paula practicing the exercise at home every day, we were ready for another exercise. I asked her to simply notice her breath as it went in and out, to focus all of her attention on where she most felt her in-breath and then focus on what it was like when she exhaled. I invited her to be aware of what it was like during those few moments, at the bottom of the out-breath, when we let go of everything. And after a while, I asked her to count the times her mind hijacked her ability to simply pay attention.

But the most important exercise was when she was able to notice her relentless inner critic passing judgment on her. So I invited her to explore this critic with curiosity. Was the voice male or female, or was it even a voice at all? What were her bodily sensations when she heard that critic? How often did that critic speak in a period of thirty minutes of observing? And when it did speak, I asked her to just listen to the voice without assuming it was true or not true. And then I instructed her to return, to notice her breath just as she had before.

Over time, Paula learned about regarding her mind with curiosity and dispassion rather than with judgment and tightness. It took us several sessions, but she was finally able to see her mind as a part of who she was (but only a part!). And when she was able to bear witness to the critical judge and not pay homage to it, she began to feel more comfortable in her skin.

Of course nothing is static, so the comfort comes and goes as does the ability to bear witness to the critical judge. But with devotion and practice, it happens more frequently. The journey can be exhilarating and it can be frustrating, depending on the day. But retraining our habitual reactions is like learning a new instrument. You can begin to enjoy the process fairly quickly, but the more you practice, the more comfortable you become with the nature of who you are and how your mind works.

In this process, Paula experienced something new—compassion for herself. There were several times when she told the story of her life and put her hand gently on her heart as she told it. It was almost as though she were holding that young girl's tender heart.

And in the process, she learned about the difference between her racing, frightened mind and her wise heart. She began to believe that there was that spark inside—believe in the wisdom that had been in there the whole time.

Though she remained terribly frightened about leaving her marriage, she knew she was going to do it. She had made up her mind. Still, another six months passed before she took any action—months when she began to understand that the fear might not ever go away and that leaving the marriage was a leap of faith. She had to have faith in that wisdom and the resilience inside of her.

When she told her husband that she was leaving the marriage, she also told him how sorry she was for both of them as she wasn't the woman he wanted and she had been unhappy for many years. And then they cried together.

At our next session, she said words I will never forget:

"I will never abandon myself again."

We humans have a tendency to abandon ourselves. After all, demands for achievement now start as early as four years old. Even if we don't have critical parents, competition and judgment begin very early. Our lives become about what we do and how well we do it. Who has time to experience the quiet voice of their heart when there is so much to do?

The world has become so loud and so demanding, we can no longer hear that still, quiet whisper that enables us to dream, to rest, to simply be with who we are. There is so much in there waiting for us to discover. Yes, we abandon ourselves. Not intentionally and not because we are neurotic, just because we are human. So many of us lose faith in our own resilience that we are more comfortable doing what we do every day even if it causes suffering—as the poet James Kavanagh said, "content with the security to know that today's suffering will be here tomorrow."[*]

But the shard of the shattered vessel is still inside. The divine spark still burns. Ultimately, even if we try to, we cannot abandon it.

I did not have to "find" that divine spark in Paula. It was there all along. She knew it was there. All I did—what we did together—was to be present in her life so that she could hear the quiet voice of her heart.

---

[*]James Kavanagh, "Freedom," in *There Are Men Too Gentle to Live Among Wolves* (Kalamazoo, Mich.: Steven J. Nash, 1991).

COMING HOME

Everybody is a genius. But if you judge a fish by its ability to climb a tree, it will live its whole life believing that it is stupid.

—Albert Einstein

Every day, I see fish who are trying to climb trees. And I was one of them. Maybe that's why, when those fish and I get together, I feel right at home.

But I'm getting ahead of myself.

First, I'd better explain why I find Einstein's quote so laugh-out-loud wise and funny and sad and true.

I had the good fortune to grow up in a two-parent home with a mother and father who loved me very much. I suspect that, as a baby, I also pleased them very much. My parents were good people who worked hard, who adored their children, and knew how to love. These were people who were raised by parents who had escaped the pogroms in Russia after facing God knows what. My grandparents expected both of my parents to make a better life for themselves, living the American dream in a post–World War II world. This dream involved pursuing success and achievement for themselves, their families, and especially their children. And their children had the same charge—to make a better life.

When I first went to kindergarten, I was very shy and nervous. Like many children, I didn't know how to make friends and just wanted to go home. And so it began. My mother, understandably, wanted me to be different, so she pushed me to make friends, telling me I had to "just go up to someone and say hello." Of course I heard this message for the next ten years of my life. In a way, I knew she was right, that I *should* be more social. And so I felt there was something wrong with me. For some reason I couldn't do whatever I was supposed to do. I couldn't be who I was supposed to be. I couldn't climb that damn tree like I should. Which made me feel ashamed of myself. Which made me more shy.

As I moved along in school, other problems arose. As early as elementary school I began to get bad grades. This was in the 1950s before we knew anything about learning disabilities, so children who got bad grades were either not very bright or just lazy. I was considered the latter. I got pushed to "study harder and concentrate" by a mother who wanted me to do better and to be better. And the more she pushed, the worse I felt about myself. I felt there was something very wrong with me, and I was ashamed.

The shame only grew when I was with my peers in school. In middle school I began to lie about my grades and tell the other kids that I had done better on my tests than I really had. Throughout high school, this was my way of getting along, always hiding my truth from the outside world. Though I had lots of friends, I always felt that if anybody really knew me, I would be humiliated or rejected somehow. I was different from the other kids, but determined I would never let them find out.

Things got even worse in college. Because my grades were so bad, I barely even got in. And when I started classes, I began struggling with my grades and had my first episode of depression. After my freshman year I was asked to leave. I went to night school after that and lived by myself in a room near St. Joseph's University in Philadelphia, where I attended school. My grades were good enough to get me into Temple University, and there I finally was adequate academically. But the feelings never went away. I felt different, *less* than everyone else.

Before long, I was no longer a child. I was a young man—but one who felt he would be okay *only* if he became a high achiever and a good family man. The problem was that I felt unworthy of true love because I was defective. But what if I was somehow able to help a woman—wouldn't she love me? So when I fell in love with Sandy, and she with me, I found someone who was as insecure as I was. But because I was four years older and already in graduate school, I became the "helper," doing everything possible to rescue her from what I thought she needed to be rescued from. I guess I felt that if I could help her, I would be okay and I would be worthy of love—that if I were a high achiever as a psychologist and had beautiful children, I would be okay. I would finally be like everyone else. I would be able to climb that tree.

None of it worked. I should have felt I had arrived, that I really was just as good as everyone else. To other people, that might even have appeared true. But it didn't feel that way to me. Though I did achieve a great deal in my profession, and I had a beautiful family and a nice home in a safe suburb, the harder I tried to climb, the more I failed to feel like I was really the equal of others. So I worked even harder at climbing. I thought if I achieved more, did more, loved more, looked better, then I would be okay. Because, God knows, I did not feel okay the way I was.

And then came the day when I knew for certain I would never be able to climb anymore. That was the day I broke my neck. Up until then, I had feared what it would be like to have all my deficits and inadequacies fully exposed. Now those fears came home to roost. After my accident, I no longer *feared* I would be unlovable. I *knew* I was. Unlovable, broken, dependent, incontinent, ugly, crippled—any humiliating word you can think of, that was me. I could no longer pretend that I could try, or even wish, to climb trees. I was there, naked—literally and metaphorically—for all the world to see.

That turned out to be the good news.

The bad news, for many of us, is that we will spend so much of our lives trying to be the person that our parents, our culture, and ultimately we ourselves feel that we could be or should be. We believe—just as I believed—that we could do better if we just tried harder. Then we will be okay. So that's what we do without ever examining what okay really means. As we try harder and never find that "okay," it's almost as though we keep going to a hardware store looking for lunch. We leave hungry . . . so we go to another hardware store!

And yes, we are hungry. We are spiritually malnourished.

So, what is the "okay" that we seek? The opposite of disease is not health, it's ease. Ultimately we are looking for a life of ease. And it begins with compassion. That little boy who was shy in kindergarten might not have been ashamed of himself if someone had sat with him who was able to feel what he felt. I still would have been shy, but I would have felt less alone, less ashamed. I'm not criticizing my parents—or any parent, for that matter. We try to do what we think will help our children in life. But my mantra for all relationships is this: Do less. Say less. Listen more and feel more. That's the ultimate display of love.

Without compassion, we carry this shame and we hide it in whatever way we can, even from ourselves. And despite our successes, that critical judge inside of us can be relentless, telling us all that we should do or be or achieve. Each day becomes an uphill battle to prove that we are not so bad or—to use Einstein's word—not so "stupid" after all.

But we can never do enough. We can never achieve enough. And somewhere, buried deep down, we know that. (And still, habits die hard: tomorrow, we might find ourselves going to the hardware store in search of our next meal!)

❀ ❀

I am reminded of a woman I treated who gave me some insight into her relationship with her mother. I often hear from women who feel they're not lovable because they're "too emotional," "too sensitive," "too tall," "too short," "too fat," or "too skinny." But in this instance, the conflict between mother and daughter focused on a different issue. The daughter was told she was "too pretty." Throughout this girl's childhood, her mother had repeatedly accused her of vanity. She called her self-centered. All the daughter cared about, according to her mother, were her looks, and no one would ever love her for who she was.

Years passed. This woman's mother has died, but the mother's judgment has not. For her whole life, this woman has been looking for security, something she never had with her parents or either of her two husbands. She has tried to be a good daughter, wife, mother, and professional. She has always believed the security she sought could be acquired from someone else—mother, father, spouse, mentor, boss. And she couldn't find it. No one delivered.

In one of our sessions, I asked her what the *experience* of security would be like. She talked about it very clearly. It was a warm feeling in the body—a feeling of resting, letting go. When you don't worry about the future and you trust it will be okay. As she went into more detail with her description, I watched her body carefully. Her breathing slowed down. In fact, *everything* seemed to slow. As she talked, her eyes actually closed. I gently pushed her to give me more and more detail, with more subtlety. I wanted to know the temperatures and sensations in every part of her body. And the more I gently probed with loving curiosity, the more I watched her settle.

When we were done with the exercise, I asked her, "What was it that you felt these last ten minutes?" She said, "I felt security." I reminded her that the feeling did not come from any of those people she had looked to for security—father, mother, husband, boss, mentor, or even therapist. It came from inside her. And I said to her, "You owe that to the child you were. You need to hold her the same way you just held yourself."

And then she said words I have never forgotten: "I feel like I *came home*."

Since then, I have that same emotional experience when I am with Joan. It's curious, because the feeling is nothing like being in the actual home I grew up in. It's not about a place, it's about an internal experience. It's a feeling that causes you to drop your

174

shoulders, rest, sometimes take a deep breath, and sometimes even cry. But it always feels safe. Home is a place where you are known for who you are and where, at this moment, anyway, everything is okay. It's something that the psychologist and Buddhist teacher Tara Brach calls "true refuge." It's a sensation of returning to yourself—returning to the child in kindergarten with compassion and love. Returning to the truth, kindness, and stability that has been there your whole life.

PRONOUNS: WHEN "THEY" BECOME "US"

I have mentioned one of the primordial-brain features that has helped us survive as a species—the way we take alarm when there are danger signals in our environment. And there's a related set of wiring that probably helped our ancestors survive. It's the way we react with caution when we encounter people who are "different." There's an alarm signal that goes off. We become wary, not knowing if that other being is safe.

You can imagine how useful that alarm might have been to our ancestors hundreds of thousands of years ago. When someone showed up from another cave or tribe, a little voice in our head said, "Be careful!" We reached for a rock or an arrow—whatever we needed to protect ourselves. We remained wary. What were the intentions of "those people"—good or ill? Could they be trusted? Or were they out to get us? We had no way of knowing whether those beings wanted to destroy us or join us. Enter the limbic system—the parts of the brain that notify the body to produce adrenaline and get ready to either throw that rock or run like hell.

That wariness remains, and we still have instincts that set off alarm bells. When we hear the phrase "you people," it is really just a socially incorrect way of saying "you are from a different tribe." But the feeling goes beyond *detection* to the question of *acceptance*. Not only is it a different tribe, it might be "a tribe I do not accept because I am still not sure it would be safe to accept your tribe as part of mine."

But what does it mean to be "other," and who is in that category? It is any group that we mark as different because of their characteristics— racial, religious, ethnic, mental, physical, or moral. It could be people with impairments or disabilities. They could be darker or lighter in complexion. They might have unfamiliar prayers, rituals, or habits. Whatever the differences, our limbic system says, "Stay away, be careful." We find safety and understanding among people like "us." We sense danger and unease when we encounter people like "them." In other words: "If we *accept* you, we might *become* like you."

People in poverty are often rejected by our society and blamed for their plight. I once did a radio show on the topic of food insecurity. This affects millions of people every day who literally don't know where their next meal is coming from. On my show I usually have one or more guests, and on this occasion I had an expert and two people who had lived with (or were still living with) food insecurity.

The reception shown to those guests by my listening audience was unlike any other I can remember during the twenty-five years my weekly show has been on the air.

During every show, I encourage callers to respond to the comments and observations of my guests. I have covered a wide range of topics and issues, and my goal, during interviews and discussions, is always to portray the humanity behind all the labels we carry. This has been my approach to topics like autism, schizophrenia, anxiety, aggression, and many more. My audience generally responds well. As evidenced by their calls, listeners appreciate the perspectives of my guests as they begin to see parts of themselves in the people I interview.

But my show on food insecurity produced a notably different pattern of responses. Many of my callers were *angry* at my guests. The implication was, anyone who struggled with issues of hunger was either lazy or not trying hard enough to make money. This was one of the few times in twenty-five years I've had callers harshly judge my guests.

Why was this "other tribe" so unacceptable? They were threatening. If we were to accept this tribe, it means we would have to accept the idea that food insecurity could happen to anyone— even us. *Oh, no,* our ego whispers, *I could not bear to live with that kind of vulnerability. I reject that, and I reject those people. I will go back to live with my secure belief that food insecurity, poverty, discrimination, or social rejection could never happen to me. If you go away, I will be able to rest in that belief whether it is true or not.* We have all sorts of mechanisms protecting us from realizing our own fragility and vulnerability. So when we see someone who is visibly vulnerable, put in this position by circumstances beyond their control, we are confronted by the truth of our lives: we are vulnerable humans at risk.

Carl Jung made the point that what we hate in others really represents parts of ourselves. He proposed that if we truly loved all parts of ourselves, we would end up hating no one. So who is "they" and who are "we"? Perhaps there is more overlap than we would be comfortable with.

Why do so many people look away when they see me in my wheelchair and pretend I'm not there? Why do people get angry at the parent of an autistic child who is out of control? I in my wheelchair and that hyperactive child are what people fear—being out of control, dependent, and vulnerable. Who has not feared all these conditions at some point in their lives? And I don't know anyone who doesn't feel great distress when they experience these fears. In order to push those emotions underground, we do the same to people who remind us of how many fears we have and how distressed we are about all of them.

Imagine this: what if we no longer feared experiencing those painful emotions? What if we no longer feared our own vulnerability? What if we were able to feel love and kindness for ourselves when we were feeling that kind of fear?

If we are able to do that, we can open our hearts and minds to our own experience. We are awake to our own suffering. And then . . .

There is a phrase that is repeated at least thirty times in the Bible. "Welcome the stranger." And of course opening your heart to the suffering of others is a central teaching in the Beatitudes of Christ.

I know, all of this sounds great, and you may even be inspired. But eventually you have to ask the question: "Sounds good, but how do we get there?"

❧ ❧

Some time ago when I was visiting Los Angeles, I stayed in a hotel that was superbly appointed, with all the elegant decorator touches that you would expect to find.

Accesswise, however, it wasn't so hot. I couldn't enter the lobby up the beautiful (but impassible) front stairs. When I asked directions, I was guided to an area near the corner of the building—obviously little-used—that doubled as a delivery point for laundry carts and food trolleys. A security gate had to be unlocked (with some difficulty) and a few items cleared away so I could make my way up the ramp leading into the lobby.

Once there, things got better, but it was obvious the hotel was not well prepared for visitors in wheelchairs. During the next few hours, as I made my way from the elevator to the handicap-accessible room, I encountered other difficulties. The sink was too low for me to get my wheelchair underneath, and there was so much furniture in the room, I couldn't get near the bed. There were many small obstacles that were easily remedied—and that could have been taken care of before I arrived. I'm sure the hotel met the code requirements, and the staff could not have been more helpful—once they were made aware of the problems—but my experience was that I felt accommodated as opposed to welcomed.

At one point I asked to meet with the manager in the lobby. As I'm sure he had done with many guests that day, he said he hoped I was enjoying my stay.

"Actually?" I said.

We got into a brief discussion. He was sincerely interested and asked whether I could take a little time to give him, essentially, a "guided tour" and show him what could be done. It would probably take a half hour or so.

I told him I couldn't do it right at that moment but suggested that we meet the next morning. He agreed, and we set a time. But before we parted, I said, "Could I ask you a question?"

"Sure," he said.

"Who in the world do you love more than anyone else?"

It didn't take him long.

"My daughter," he replied.

"Okay, could you do this before we meet tomorrow morning? Imagine that your daughter is visiting your hotel."

"Okay."

"And she's in a wheelchair."

We did meet the next morning, but we didn't need to. He didn't need my input anymore. Imagining his daughter in a wheelchair, he had seen what it was like. Maybe he had even felt what it was like. He knew what had to be done.

I knew what had changed for him. When he spoke with me, he was speaking with a guest in a wheelchair. I was one of "them." But when he looked through the eyes of someone he loved—the eyes of his own daughter—that was "us." When "they" become "us," it makes our world gentler and larger. Embracing the "other" is the best way to discover well-being, kindness, and the wisdom we're born with.

THAT SPARK

When the phone rang, I saw by the caller ID that it was a patient of mine I hadn't seen in many years. I had first met Linda's husband, Len, about twenty years before. At the time, he was in his mid-fifties and was unhappy with his career as a physician. Len had loved his career until managed-care took over and he began to feel like a bureaucrat who just had occasional patient contact. The reason he had became a doctor in the first place was to help people—and in the managed-care system he now he felt he was helping line the pockets of CEOs.

Len had also been distressed in his marriage. Both he and his wife—a public school teacher—had been working ever-longer hours in jobs that were less than gratifying. Both were disappointed with their careers and were stressed with the day-to-day work. They were tired physically and emotionally. As a result they were drifting apart.

I had worked with Len for several months and had helped him make some difficult decisions about giving up his practice and joining a hospital group where he would be on salary. But throughout I remained concerned about his marriage, because I know that the quality of someone's marriage has a major impact on their mood and outlook. So when things had settled down for Len in his new position, I asked him how he would feel about changing directions a bit and inviting Linda to join us. He readily agreed.

When Linda arrived she looked like a beaten-down woman. There were circles under her eyes, her complexion was pallid, and she walked with her shoulders curled over—a classic sign of depression.

Both were angry at each other but not fully aware of it. What they were aware of was that they had little or no interest in spending time with each other. Eventually, as they admitted their anger, it also became clear that each felt abandoned by the other.

The work was difficult. Both partners were deeply hurt and protected themselves by taking a stance of righteous indignation. However, once the room began to feel safe, they began to open more to where the pain really was. Instead of blaming each other, they were able to express their varying degrees of sadness or fear or loneliness.

During the sessions of marital therapy, everything had worked out pretty well. They finally realized how important they were to each other and, in time, recognized that the reason they were angry in the first place was because they needed to be closer. We talked a good deal about love and why they loved each other. More important, we talked about *how* they loved each other and what could be done to help them love each other better, more consciously, more generously, and more selflessly. It took practice, but we got there. For Len and Linda the therapy was over at that point.

But not for the family as a whole. Over the years, there was difficulty with their adult children. A great deal of conflict arose between the son and the father, so I got to work with the two of them. I helped them understand one another and the nature of the conflict. Several years later, Linda felt her daughter was getting depressed, so I saw her also.

It was almost like I had become the family psychologist. And because of that, I became very fond of each member of this family.

�

When I picked up the phone, Linda's voice sounded distressed. "Things are very bad with Len, and I need to come in and talk about it." She went on to tell me that Len had become quite ill very suddenly. Tests revealed he had pancreatic cancer.

"I am losing my husband and I need help getting through it," said Linda.

I saw Linda a few times, but she had difficulty coming in regularly because of Len's medical appointments. I asked whether Len was physically able to come in, but when Linda hesitated and said, "I think he's just too frail, but I know he would benefit from seeing you," I offered to go to their home to meet with Len.

When I arrived, both of their children were present. They had come home frequently over the previous few weeks as their father's condition deteriorated.

It had been a long time since I had been with the children. Now they were middle-aged, with children of their own. Though it was wonderful to see them again, they both looked tired and worried. While Linda prepared Len to come downstairs, I talked with the adult children who expressed their great concern for both of their parents. Richard cried as he said he couldn't bear to see his father suffering.

After about twenty minutes, Linda came into the room pushing a very emaciated man in a wheelchair. He had a nasal cannula attached to oxygen. I felt so sad. Len had always been very powerful and clear-minded, and I had so enjoyed working with him. Though we had dealt with some difficult and painful issues in therapy, we had also enjoyed the banter between us. But now there was no banter in this man. He labored for each breath.

Linda also looked exhausted. Despite her smile and air of competence, I knew she had most of the responsibility for her husband's care and I could see that she was running out of steam. Yet she was afraid to allow anyone else to care for her beloved husband, knowing their time together was limited.

Len said he wanted to talk with me privately. Linda helped Len into a lounge chair, covered him with a blanket, and then she and the children left the room. Once they were gone, it became clear why Len wanted to speak to me privately. He wanted to protect his family from all his fears. He told me he was terrified of dying. When I asked him details, he said he was afraid that he would spend eternity in some kind of darkness. He asked me what I thought happened when we die, and I told him I thought it might be emptiness, but that I wouldn't care much because "I'll be dead!" (I carefully calculated my humor here as I thought it was important to help Len get some perspective. Not only that, laughter is so healthy for mind and body.)

I told Len that the real pain of dying is usually not where we're going but more about what we're losing. When he thought about all his accomplishments and all the people he had helped, he realized that the great pain of dying would be losing the love of his family.

After my meeting with Len, he needed a few hours' rest. Then the whole family gathered together in the living room. At first, we sat quietly for a few minutes, knowing this time together would be difficult and precious as everyone felt such deep love and sadness. I asked Len to repeat for his family what he had said earlier to me about his greatest pain. As everyone wept, he talked about his regret: that he worked too many hours and hadn't spent enough time with his family. He said that he had never been able to express his love adequately as he never was good at expressing emotions. He wanted them to know how grateful he was, being surrounded by this wonderful family, and how proud he was of every one of them.

And, one by one, each of them talked about what Len meant to them. Richard talked about the guidance he'd received from his father—that he would carry with him for the rest of his life and share with his own children. Through tears, he went across the room and hugged his father. His daughter said that throughout her childhood she always wanted to be married to a man who loved her as much as he loved Linda. At this point, all of us were crying. Linda said nothing as she and Len gazed into each other's eyes, the look of people deeply in love getting ready to say good-bye to each other.

Len was exhausted and went to bed shortly after the meeting. I chatted with the family briefly, and when I returned home, there was an e-mail from Linda saying that Len wanted to speak with me. When I heard his voice on the telephone, it sounded weaker than before, but he also seemed calmer. He said, "A strange thing happened after our session. Somehow the darkness of death feels less frightening. Much more sad, but less scary. It feels as though something will continue after I am gone. Love. Their love for me will continue and I have no idea, but perhaps my love for them will continue also. I find peace in that."

We met one more time as a family the following week. This time Len was in a wheelchair, and a nurse from hospice was nearby, in constant attendance. But when we met, the air was lighter even though the end was closer. Len said that as he had thought about it during the previous few months, he realized all he had ever wanted in life was to be able to care for his family, help give them some semblance of stability, and be able to love all three of them and have them love him. He said he wished he had known that that was his priority forty years earlier.

At which point I reminded him that he had everything he ever wanted right there, that very moment. And despite how he felt or what his future might portend, that moment could be one of the best of his life.

And the spark was there, in that room. The one in each of us, that divine wisdom placed inside before we are born, so often forgotten or hidden, but always there. The spark, kindled by love, that arrives before we are born and does not leaves us until well after our death.

AFTERWORD

I received my first Social Security check in June the year I finished writing this book. It was pretty surprising because it seemed like just a few years earlier that I received my final high school report card! More than fifty years seemed to have passed in a moment. And then I remembered waiting for my seventeenth birthday so I could get my driver's license. Those six months before I turned seventeen felt like a half century! To a young man, time creeps slowly. But to an old man, time whizzes by at frightening speed. How can that be when the clock moves at exactly the same speed throughout our life cycle? Is it possible to somehow slow down time? Actually, it is.

So what now? I'm sixty-seven years old, and I have a terminal illness called life. As I watch the seasons change, my most fervent

wish is to see the next season and then the next. I make no prom-
ises to be a better person, to eat better, or to go to synagogue more.
The only promise I make is to try to notice those seasons in as
much detail, with as much gratitude, as I can muster, knowing I
may not see that season again. And as every season changes, I look
to the resilience of my body, my spirit, and the love of my friends
and family and whisper, "Thank you. Thank you."

Between my meditation practice and all of the weeks and
months I have stayed in bed looking out the window, I have come
to appreciate the way some trees sway in a gentle breeze and how
many shades of green there are in the summer. These are things I
never noticed when I was younger, but now I do. And in that noticing, time seems to slow down.

In this book I've talked a great deal about well-being, internal security, and faith in our own humanity. But even those things come
and go.

So what can we hold on to? Well, my Buddhist teacher would
say we cannot hold on to anything. Never a big fan of any ortho-
doxy, I'm thinking, "Okay, that might work for you, but I don't
see that working for this neurotic Jewish kid from Atlantic City!"

I don't want to conclude this book sounding like a romantic
musical number, but after sixty-seven years of life—thirty-three
of which I have observed from my stainless-steel perch—I have
discovered that what gives us stability is love.

The lesson we learned from Len in the previous chapter is a
universal one. At the end of his life he finally realized that all he
ever really wanted was love—to love and to be loved. And when
we approach the end of our lives, magically our clock slows down

and we realize what's always been important to us. Somehow we acquire that precious docket of wisdom we knew when we were children, that love will nurture our selves and give our lives meaning. Not money, looks, power, or even achievements. All of those things bring temporary happiness.

When we allow ourselves to love who we love—and experience that in every cell of our bodies—time slows down. When we have the courage to feel the love of others and let that love penetrate our very being, it brings warmth and stability to our lives.

My God, I love this life. And how deeply I wish the same for you.

ACKNOWLEDGMENTS

Everything starts with Ed Claflin, my agent, my muse, and my dear, dear friend of over twenty years. Without his talent and guidance, none of my books would ever have been written.

Dr. Michael Baime runs the University of Pennsylvania Program for Mindfulness. I first met him nearly twenty years ago when he became my teacher, my guide, and my mentor. And now he's one of my closest friends. Through his teachings I have learned to take a step back from my own mind and observe it with curiosity and compassion.

I am so very grateful to have been hosting "Voices in the Family" (WHYY.org/voices) for twenty-eight years. And over those years, I have met some of the best and brightest minds in this country and beyond. More people than I can count went from being guests on my show to becoming dear friends—among them, Jon Kabat-Zinn, Dan Gilbert, Dan Siegel, Tara Brach, Kristin Neff, Sharon Salzberg, Rick Hanson, Amishi Jha, and dozens more.

My amazing daughters Ali and Debbie, both wonderful women, are making the world a better place in their own way. I feel pride and gratitude every day when I think about them.

My biological grandson, Sam, is one of the most extraordinary people of any age I have ever met. Before he could speak, he was more compassionate than most, more kind than most, and more generous of spirit than most. From the time he was very young, he approached everything with a curious mind and an open heart. Sam is now thirteen years old, and none of these attributes has changed. He is one of the best teachers I have ever encountered. Sam and I love each other very much, but he has no idea how honored I am to be his grandfather.

My sweet five-year-old Jacob is my grandson in every way but biologically. His eyes shine, his heart is open, his mind is hungry to learn and learn, and he is so easy to love. Jacob is one of my great teachers and my best playmate.

Joan Kaczmarski entered my life about four years ago and has become, in the deepest sense, a true companion. Throughout the writing of the book she has held me, literally and metaphorically, as I ruminate about ideas, second-guess my language, burst through with excitement, weep with joy or sadness—you know, standard writer's stuff! I am so deeply grateful for her support.

ABOUT THE AUTHOR

Daniel Gottlieb, a practicing psychologist and family therapist, is the host of "Voices in the Family" on WHYY, Philadelphia's National Public Radio affiliate. From 1993 until 2008, he wrote a highly regarded column for the *Philadelphia Inquirer* called "Inside Out," reflecting his perspective on world events and the ways we experience them. Author of five books, including the bestselling *Letters to Sam* and *Learning from the Heart*, columnist, and radio host, Gottlieb also lectures locally and nationally on topics related to personal and social well-being, helping individuals and families find a greater sense of fulfillment and community.

The author's royalties from sales of this book will be donated to the Khulani Special School, Mduku Community, Kwazulu Natal, South Africa. For more information about the school, please go to www.DrDanGottlieb.com.